Through the Eyes
of an
Orphan

MY YEARS AT MILTON HERSHEY SCHOOL:
STUMBLING BLOCK OR STEPPING STONE

P.D. Hilary

ISBN 978-1-64028-385-5 (Paperback)
ISBN 978-1-64028-639-9 (Hard Cover)
ISBN 978-1-64028-386-2 (Digital)

Christian Faith Publishing, Inc.
296 Chestnut Street
Meadville, PA 16335
www.christianfaithpublishing.com

Scripture taken from the King James Version. Public domain.

Printed in the United States of America

Contents

Introduction

One of my earliest childhood memories was when I was looking out the window at the end of the upstairs hallway around the age of four. I must have gotten up early from a nap, and the house was so quiet and still. As I looked out the window, I saw no one. I felt everyone had left me, and this feeling of horror came over me. I cried and cried until someone came and got me. This memory of feeling abandoned that day has stayed with me all of my life.

This is a true story of how that feeling became a reality when both my parents passed away. It is a journey of the feeling of abandonment that came true and turned to bitterness over what would happen to me, and how God would turn my journey into a great blessing because of the life lessons I learned along the way.

I would cry many times in my life after that day. I looked out the upstairs hallway window at a world I did not understand. Maybe, just maybe, you will relate in some way to my journey, and the lessons learned may be of some help to you in your journey. It is a journey of inner struggle to know oneself and find purpose and a place in that world outside the upstairs hallway window.

Ultimately, years later, after the last page of this book, this path would lead me to God, and I would find great purpose in life and use these lessons today. If this book is a help to you and the lessons I learned strengthen your journey or lead you to God, then I have accomplished one of the purposes of writing this story. Everyone has a story. These are the lessons learned about life *Through the Eyes of an Orphan*.

Dedication

To my grandson, Sawyer, who, at the age of eight, stayed over at our house and said, "Papa, tell me an orphanage story," which encouraged me to put these stories on paper. To my other grandchildren—Larynn, Clay, Wayde David, and Wesly—who I hope will enjoy the life lessons.

To Pastor Ken Kistler, Pastor Jeff Gwilt, Pastor Todd Wentworth, and Pastor Jeff Hurst who inspired me to write these 40,000 words, which I was not sure I could write. To my daughter, Rachelle Emmett, and her husband, Joe, for the blessing they are to me and whom I am so proud of. Most of all, to my wife Bonnie whom I love deeply and who has been my confidant all these years.

CHAPTER 1

Early Memories

My parents on their wedding day. Their chance meeting
when he was getting off work at Armco Steel and she
was getting off the bus to walk home from work. He
offered her a ride. This union would forge my destiny.

I do not have many early childhood memories, but there was one night when I was extremely afraid. I felt sure that there were snakes under my bed. Another time I stood at the end of our upstairs hallway looking out the window thinking everyone had left me. I cried so much! Another time I was so puzzled when I walked into the bathroom and saw the bathtub covered in blood. It made an impression on me that has stayed with me all these years. I was around four years old, and although the impression bothered me, at that moment I did not understand the devastating meaning of the bathtub covered in blood, nor did I ask.

When I was four years old, I was sleeping in my parents' room. I woke up, and someone was calling for my dad. He did not respond because he had died in the night. At the time, I did not understand... I only remember being there. My last memory of him was when we visited the funeral home. All of this happened when I was four years old or younger. Years later, I understood the blood in the tub and what happened that morning in the bedroom. My father died of alcoholism, and the blood in the tub was from cirrhosis of the liver. But at the time it happened, all I knew was that I woke up and I was fatherless.

Years went by as my mother tried to rear three boys on her own. As I grew, obviously, so did my memory of my early childhood. My memories were mostly good, some funny, a few were sad. I remember playing kick the can and football with the neighbor kids. Sometimes, we would have a neighborhood softball game involving the adults as well as the kids. When I was seven years old, I told my mom I was going to run away. I do not know why. My mom was a good mom. She brought down a suitcase and suggested that I pack. I cried. That was the last time I ever suggested something like that. I always felt loved by my mom even though my memories of her are few.

My mom could be tough. She was rearing three boys, and my oldest brother, Bob, was hard to handle. As I sat at the table one day, he talked back to her. She tossed a plate like a Frisbee and hit him right above the eye. One day, I decided to shave. I thought it was a good idea; however, my mother did not. When I was caught, which is something rather consistent for the rest of my life, she broke off a willow branch from the tree in our front yard. With one hand, she held my arm; and with the other, she switched me. I deserved every bit of it.

It is funny how life teaches us lessons—even at an early age—that stick with us for a lifetime. At another time, when I was around seven years old, our neighborhood was playing a softball game together with kids and adults. I think it was the first time I realized how painfully shy I am. I remember how I wanted to play but could not get the courage to ask.

Finally, I mustered up the courage to go up to a man and ask, "Can I play?"

I remember it like yesterday.

He said, "I am sorry, son. The game is over."

Oh how crushed I was: I had waited too long and had missed the opportunity. That handicap of shyness has plagued me for many years and in many ways.

Does shyness handicap you? How many *games* have you missed that have left a stinging scar because you were afraid to step up, speak up, or risk failure? Shyness must be overcome in our lives and be replaced with a bold humility. It was years later when I came to Christ and through His strength began to overcome the restricting powers of shyness so as to finally get in the ballgame. Two verses helped me to overcome shyness. "For God hath not given us the spirit of fear; but of power, and of love, and of a sound mind" (2 Tim. 1:7), and "I can do all things through Christ which strengtheneth me" (Phil. 4:13). Those simple words I can recall to remind myself of their promises, even by counting the words on my fingers. Please do not miss the game of life like I did because of shyness. You must overcome your shyness and get in the game before the game is over. I have heard it said, "Most people die with the music still inside of them." Get it out before it is too late, the song is over, and your life is done. By God's grace I have been trying to do that.

When I turned eight years old, my life was about to take a drastic change. It would scar me and eventually bless my life forever. I did not fully understand the seriousness of the situation, but my mom had become ill. We moved from our house to live with my Aunt Theresa and Uncle Chuck so that they could care for my mom. Theresa was my mother's sister. I never heard the word *cancer* before. One morning, in June 1960, my aunt woke me up, sat me on the couch, put her arm around me, and told me my mother had passed away. That is how I became an orphan. I woke up one day when I was four years old and my father was gone; and one day when I was eight years old, my mother was gone. My life would never be the same. I felt like I was going into a dark tunnel. The Bible says we do not know what a day brings forth. How true that was for me, and I was not prepared.

In one day, our life can change through a death, a divorce, an accident, a sickness, or other tragedy. Often, there is no stopping it as in my case. It just happens, and you are left to deal with it. It can result in anger, bitterness, and hatred toward people, life in general, and ultimately God. All this happened to me, which brought on what God calls "the years of the locust"—years filled with bitterness, anger, and hatred. This can lead to sin against God in thousands of ways and wasted years. As I share in these pages, I will try to speak as honestly and as frankly as I can. You will see a change and a difference at my lowest point, when at twenty-three years of age, God redeemed my soul and reclaimed my year of the locust through the dramatic salvation of my soul. I found it to be the only hope for what a day brings forth. I face life differently now—with hope. This is how I cope with life and face each new day.

- I bask in the love of God's forgiveness.
- I appreciate every day, trying to live it to the fullest.
- I have learned to serve God and my fellow man out of love and not for selfish reasons.

- I try not only to appreciate life, but to enjoy it and not put on my rain coat until the storm comes.
- I have learned how to accept the tragedy of my past as blessings for God's glory because of His grace.
- I have learned that God is sovereign, and He has a plan for my life—past, present, and future. Nothing will happen to me outside of His sovereign will.
- I am working on the fact that death will be my friend, as my wife wrote in a poem, "Death Is My Passport to Thee." When my work here on earth is done and God tarries, I will go home to be with Him.

"Death"

What is death?
A disappearance of breath,
A heart full of sorrow,
A loss of tomorrow,
An empty chair,
So hard to bear,
A broken heart,
Torn apart.

Why is death?
Why the pain that so remains?
Why the tears,
Why not cheers?
Why disbelief?
Why God, why, so much grief?
Why the young and why the old?
To this the answer is not told.

So help me God, help me to see,
That death is my passport to thee.

—By Bonnie Heist Maitland

Bonnie who became the love of my life and a great
encourager in my journey — love at first sight for me.

Where would I go? What would happen to me? Where would I live? Who wants an eight-year-old orphan? No one, when you really think about it. Babies can be adopted quickly, but an eight-year-old boy is not a hot commodity—not even to the extended family. All of these decisions were outside of my control. I went from relative to relative—sometimes a month at a time. Each day was a day of uncertainty, and nothing seemed to make sense. I guess I was waiting for someone somewhere to make a decision. That decision, when it came, changed my life forever. Movies are made about a little man behind a curtain with a booming voice pulling levers or a man pulling the strings behind the scenes as one would pull the strings of a marionette puppet that seems to affect the destiny of many lives. Who really does these things, and where do they get their power? Who was doing this? To my surprise, I would meet Him years later when I was twenty-three years old. One lonely night, we would come face-to-face in a spiritual sense. He offered no apologies for allowing my life to be altered in such a fashion. I understand and appreciate now what He chose to allow in my life. The little man I thought was behind the curtain was God Himself—the Sovereign Ruler of the universe who pulled back the curtain and revealed Himself to me the night when I accepted Jesus Christ as my Savior.

As I began my journey as an orphan, I remembered being at Aunt Ann and Uncle Floyd Henricks' house. Tim and Dave were their sons, and Dorothy was their daughter. We boys shoveled chicken manure. What a dirty job, but oh how we laughed and had fun! We worked for money—not much, but it was the first time I had ever gotten paid. I had my own money. My stay there did not last long.

The Henricks had a cow that stepped on my foot, which left a lasting impression on my mind. We would laugh at night until their mother would come upstairs. She was so sweet and loving. If we continued, Uncle Floyd came into the bedroom, and all laughter ceased. He was a great guy but he was firm—fair and serious.

I had learned to drive a lawnmower at Uncle Floyd and Aunt Ann's house. I mowed the grass, which was exciting for me as an eight-year-old boy. All of my family members were hard workers, and I enjoyed helping them. I made a mistake by trying to put the mower in the garage after I was finished mowing. I should have stopped while I was ahead. When I pulled into the garage, I got scared. I pushed the gas pedal instead of the brake. I smashed the lawnmower into Uncle Floyd's work bench. I was mortified! It revealed two things about me. I was not good under pressure because I got scared and pushed the gas pedal instead of the brake. Secondly, I did not like conflict, and in my fear of man—specifically Uncle Floyd—I did not confess. Of course, I got caught! I should have learned that lesson before it became the pattern for the rest of my life: I always got caught. I have come to realize that getting caught has been a blessing in my life. It is the sign that Someone loves me, Someone is watching me, and Someone is trying to help me to do right so that I will not continue in secret sin. Fair but gracious Uncle Floyd helped me to get back on track. Years later when I came to Christ, that truth of being honest—

especially when wrong has occurred—has become an anchor for me. My stay at the Henricks' lasted about four months.

Next, I journeyed onto a farm of my Uncle Johnny and my Aunt Catherine Erdos. Johnny was my mother's brother, and although he scared me, I came to appreciate him. He was my first contact with a backslapping Baptist. He always talked loud and seemed like he was yelling. He was always quoting Scripture and talking about God. What I really liked about him was his breakfast of onions and eggs. I also learned how to take the innards out of chickens after he cut off their heads to butcher them. They lived in an old farmhouse with a lot of creaks and noises, but I felt a lot of love when I was there.

My Aunt Catherine was sweet and wonderful like my mother. Although she was crippled in the hands with rheumatoid arthritis, she was always happy. I heard her say, "Oh Johnny" when her husband was quirky or ranting and raving about how bad the world was and how God was unhappy. My Aunt Catherine loved the Lord and had such a sweet, inoffensive way about her.

Cousins Marybeth, Phil, Johnny Jr., and I did silly things like make perfume from rose petals to sell, or Johnny Jr. would do a flip out of the barn loft and land on his feet. Sometimes we did bad things like putting gas in squirt bottles, squirting each other, and lighting it. It would burn off quickly, but it was not a smart thing to do. We would ride our bikes to the swimming hole just like the Norman Rockwell painting.

The first time I realized I was jumpy was when we were going to the swimming hole and I was riding on the back of someone's bike. A big truck came by and honked its horn. It scared me so badly that I clamped my feet together and the spokes ripped the heels right off my shoes. I have been jumpy ever since! It was quite an experience for an eight-year-old boy.

Those were great carefree, happy days—not knowing what was coming in the near future. Although it was a time of uncertainty in my life, I was the honored guest in each home. Soon my life would change, but now it was off to another relative's house. My Uncle Joe and Aunt Jean Erdos had two boys about my age, and we had a wonderful time. Uncle Joe was my mom's brother. Although it did not mean much, I thought they were wealthy because they lived in a large house and had their own swimming pool. It was like a vacation at a resort. Larry, Darrell, and I got along great. Uncle Joe owned his own furniture store and was a self-made man because he had done extremely well in business. His sons would follow him later in the furniture business, and they did well also.

CHAPTER 2

"And Now to the Issue of the Boys"

I overheard talk at times of what they were going to do with me. Who *they* were, I was not quite sure. I did hear that Aunt Jean and Uncle Joe were talking about adopting me, but it never happened. I am not sure why it never happened; but in the end, it turned out the best for me.

Life has a funny way of doing that since God is in control. For me, He had a different path. I would someday travel to the beat of a different drum. It would take many years for me to understand why. It was not ready to take shape, but something I would later begin to describe as a *call of destiny* occurred, even though for many years I could not explain what that was. Later when that call became clear, I had an interesting conversation with my Uncle Joe. I was twenty-five years old at the time. I told him of my calling to become a pastor and go into the ministry. He felt I had too much talent to do that and could do better for myself otherwise. He was not saved at the time, but came to know the Lord later. I am sure he rejoiced in the choice I made after he was saved.

It is interesting that at eight years old, everybody made my decisions for me; and at twenty-five years old, God made the decision for me—my life's call to the ministry. My ministry of thirty-five years has been the greatest blessing to me. I learned the important lesson that when I was eight-years-old and it seemed that everyone was making decisions for me, it was really God directing behind the scenes.

My next stop was at my Uncle George, who was my mother's brother, and Aunt Helen Erdos' house, which was my first experience with sternness, which I would become well acquainted with in the orphanage. Once I had to clean my plate, and I had a great battle with a slice of tomato. I was told to eat it, but I just could not. So I sat at the table staring at the slice of tomato for hours. It became such an issue that the more I sat, the more dread welled up inside of me. It was horrible and is still etched in my mind. Finally, the oldest son, Richard, had compassion on me and began to be my cheerleader. At every difficult point in my life—no matter how great or small—even before I was saved, someone would come along at the right moment and have compassion on me, encourage me, believe in me, and challenge me to rise above.

My cousin, Richard, said, "You can eat this tomato. Repeat after me. 'I like tomatoes' again and again."

I said it as I gagged each piece down until it was all gone. What a dreadful experience! Even today, I usually give my wife my tomatoes from my salad or sandwich, but I like tomato sauce, salsa, and—of all things—toasted tomato sandwiches.

The worst memory at Uncle George's home came when we were playing in the basement with arrows. Someone dared me to throw an arrow at them. I gently tossed it toward one of the kids. As I remember, it hardly came out of my hand. One of my cousins ran upstairs and said I had thrown an arrow at him. I was locked in a closet for what seemed like an eternity. It was dark, and I wept and wept. It was the first time I was ever accused of something I did not feel I had done. It was a horrible feeling: I remember feeling hurt and angry. It surely would not be the last time—especially since I was heading for the orphanage, which I did not know at the time. I love my Uncle George and Aunt Helen who have since passed away, but that was my last experience at their house. I was scared of them for many years, but I came to love them.

My first feelings of abandonment, rejection, and attack at my self-worth came when my mother died. I was introduced to an unfair world for the first time. I had feelings of rejection, which I later came to know as bitterness. I was introduced to the bitterness of life. There would be happy days, but this thread would run through my life and grow into a hangman's noose when I was twenty-three years old. Only the Lord could take it from my neck and make me a free man. The orphanage would provide much rope for that. One of the great principles of life that began at this time and was confirmed by the time I graduated from the orphanage is that life is not fair. You may have found that out in your life, and if not, you will. Once you have experienced it, you will also experience its by-products of bitterness, anger, and even hatred. There is a way out, and I hope that this book, in the end, brings hope.

I spent a short time at my Aunt Josephine and Uncle Joe Nemeth's home. (I could always say I had a Joe Nemeth in the family). Joe was a fisherman and a nice guy. Aunt Phennie, as we called her, was my mother's sister. She was a large lady and always hugged and kissed me and called me "Davey." It stuck in the family. Even today, if I hear the word "Davey" and I turn around, I know it has to be someone in my family. Even when I was out of high school and went to family reunions, there would be Aunt Phennie. When she saw me, she would cry "Davey" and open her arms, and I would disappear. She would kiss me with those wet kisses and make a big fuss over me. I loved it. She loved my mom and would always be at the family gatherings.

Her daughter, Theresa Ann, and I were close, but I know I was always a little brat bugging her. We are still close today, and she has become one of my greatest supporters just like her mom. Aunt Phennie was good at cooking and hugging. She cared for her father, my grandpa, but I only knew him briefly before he died. He was my only grandparent I ever met. That is when I realized I was Hungarian, for he came from the old country. He was big on halupkis and big on family because he had a large family and, best of all, my mother. Years later, I realized how important family is, how ethnicity affected me, and what it means to have a great heritage as I have become a grandfather.

I stayed for a short time with my Uncle Louie and Aunt Elizabeth Erdos. Uncle Louie, my mother's brother, was a big man with a booming voice. I liked him, but I sensed he was a no-nonsense type of guy. Two of his boys, Sonny and Tom, became all-American swimmers as well as college coaches in later years. The one fact that may have changed my life with Uncle Louie and Aunt Elizabeth was that they were my godparents. I was born into a Roman Catholic family, and if anything happened to my parents, Louie was supposed to become my guardian. That did not happen, and I am not sure why. Instead, I heard that they were going to place me in a Catholic orphanage. It is funny how life has a lot of twists and turns.

So I ended up at my Aunt Theresa's and Uncle Chuck's home. They had cared for my mother when she was dying. They reared two girls, Gayle and Jan, with whom I became close. I am glad God is sovereign because I had no control over my life at this time. After being passed around the family, this is the family with whom I landed. My aunt was a beautiful woman, and her hair and dress were always picture perfect. She was always nurturing me, feeding me, and hugging me. She had many opinions on many things. We are close to this day, and I still call her "Ma." I would tease her sometimes for fun and sometimes for survival because of those strong Hungarian opinions. She was my mother's sister and was intensely loyal. She was a real Martha, like in the Bible, always helping others.

My uncle was of a different sort—probably the fairest and toughest guy I know. I cannot explain it, but even at eight years old, it did not take me long to figure him out. I did not have problems with Uncle Chuck. He spoke, and I listened. He did not say much, but when he did, it was always filled with truth, fairness, and wisdom. He would say something, and it was up to me to figure out the meaning and application. Over the next twelve years, this was my home base for vacations from the orphanage and for a short time after I graduated.

PITTSBURGH NATIONAL BANK
BUTLER OFFICE
BUTLER, PENNSYLVANIA

July 8, 1960

The future welfare of the boys will be somewhat determined by the housing we can provide. Our Trust Committee has agreed that we should expend $30.00 per month for each boy wherever they are living. Robert of course will get well and he may choose to live wherever he pleases, but on Francis and David I would appreciate any suggestions that you may have. I understand that each of you in your individual families have the normal situations that may not be conducive to helping the boys. On the other hand, while they may stay where they are for the next couple of months, some other plan might be even better, and if you have any ideas, please send them on to me.

According to my present schedule I would like to get the above problems pretty well worked out by the 22nd of July. Please feel free to write or call at my office on this or any other matter.

Yours very truly

Mitchell G. Uram
Trust Officer

mgu:om

The Letter of July 8, 1960

In 2014 a letter was passed on to me by a family member who had received it from my mother's sister, Ann Henricks, who had kept it all these years. It had been fifty-four years since the letter was written. The letter was addressed to Ann from Mitch Uram, the Bank Trust Officer at Pittsburgh National Bank, who handled my family's affairs after my parents passed away. This letter was mostly about settling my family's estate, but a paragraph of the letter indicated that my future as an eight-year-old boy was *up for grabs*. My life could have looked so much differently today depending on the direction it had taken back then. At the date of that letter, my future was up in the air, and God's destiny in my life had not yet been revealed. The next-to-the-last paragraph of the letter read as follows:

The future welfare of the boys will be somewhat determined by the housing we can provide. Our Trust Committee has agreed that we should expend $30 per month for each boy wherever they are living. Robert, of course, will get well and he may choose to live wherever he pleases, but on Francis and David I would appreciate any suggestions that you may have. I understand that each of you in your individual families have the normal situations that may not be conducive to helping the boys. On the other hand, while they may stay where they are for the next couple of months, some other plan might be even better, and if you have any ideas, please send them on to me.

The fate of my future seemed to lie in Mitch Uram's hands. He was the one who recommended a place called Milton Hershey School, saying it might be the best place for me. It was a school with 1,500 boys in it. If I could get in and pass the physical, academics, and other evaluations, I would stay there until I graduated from high school. I would come home for Christmas, Easter, and summer vacation every year for the next nine years until I graduated. Bob, my oldest brother, was eighteen years old, and he seemed to be ready to be out on his own. Fran, my other brother, was fifteen years old, and I was eight years old. Thirty dollars a month was offered if someone would take us in. I know there were those who wanted to help Fran and me, but they had their own families so no one could take us in permanently. This was the time period when I went from house to house during the summer of 1960.

To find this out after fifty-four years gave me an insight on that twilight time between my mother's death and when I went to Hershey. I am amazed at the sovereignty of God in all things. My future was up in the air and spread out in a letter to one of my aunts. I guess, at first, there was sadness that no one could take in an eight-year-old orphaned boy. It was my destiny. My life would have been different if someone would have taken me. God wanted me, not my brothers, to go to Hershey. He had a special plan for me, and while I have always felt that in my life since my mother died, I did not know how to explain it until I became a Christian.

Before I tell you how the decision was made for me to go to Hershey, I am reminded of my favorite poem I learned years later.

"The Touch of the Master's Hand"

'Twas battered and scarred, and the auctioneer
    Thought it scarcely worth his while
To waste much time on the old violin,
    But held it up with a smile.
"What am I bidden, good folks," he cried,
    "Who'll start the bidding for me?"
"A dollar, a dollar. Then two! Only two?
    Two dollars, and who'll make it three?"
"Three dollars, once; three dollars, twice; going for three;
    Going for three..." But no,
From the room, far back, a grey-haired man
    Came forward and picked up the bow;
Then wiping the dust from the old violin,
    And tightening the loosened strings,
He played a melody pure and sweet,
    As a caroling angel sings.

The music ceased, and the auctioneer,
    With a voice that was quiet and low,
Said: "What am I bid for this old violin?"
    And he held it up with the bow.
"A thousand dollars, and who'll make it two?
    Two thousand! And who'll makes it three?
Three thousand, once; three thousand, twice,
    And going and gone," said he.

The people cheered, but some of them cried,
    "We do not quite understand.
What changed its worth?" Swift came the reply:
    "The touch of the Master's hand."
And many a man with life out of tune,
    And battered and scarred with sin,
Is auctioned cheap to a thoughtless crowd
    Much like that old violin.

A "mess of pottage," a glass of wine,
    A game—and he travels on.
He is "going" once, and "going" twice,
    He's "going" and almost "gone."
But the Master comes, and the foolish crowd
    Never can quite understand
The worth of a soul and the change that is wrought
    By the touch of the Master's hand.

—By Myra Brooks Welch (1877-1959)
(Source: www.allpoetry.com, 2016)

I know I was only eight years old, but I was like the old violin. I had no idea where I would end up. The events seemed to unfold like this.

Some time after July 8, 1960, Mr. Uram came to believe that Milton Hershey School would be the best place for me. I was too young to understand what was going on at eight years of age, but there was a lot of adult talk. A family meeting was called at Theresa Ann's house where all of my mother's siblings met to decide what to do with me. They discussed the situation that my brother Bob had become wild in his lifestyle and that my brother Fran had become wild also. The consensus was that I would probably head the same way, and they felt the suggestion of Mitch Uram to have me go to Hershey was the best decision for me.

I know my family loved me and could not take me in. They were right: I needed something more like the old violin in the poem. Mr. Uram and my family were not just doing their job: they were instruments in God's hand. I believe that God loves to work this way—like the old violin on the auction block in the poem. Do I hear $30 a month for this orphan boy? Anybody, anybody, and God said, "I will take him. I have great plans for this boy. Place him at Milton Hershey School for me so that I can begin his training for a life I have in store for him. I will take him from that auction block and someday use him to spread my gospel as a preacher. He is a wild root right now, and he will need the discipline that Hershey will provide; however, when I break his will someday, he will play sweet music for me like *The Old Violin*." I cannot tell you how grateful, humbled, and blessed I am that God loves me so. I know that God was working behind the scenes when that letter was written. Mr. Uram found out about Milton Hershey and my family had the meeting that would change my life forever.

L—Aunt Theresa (Ma)
R—Trust officer Mitch Uram
I am smiling because I did not know I was staying, thus the
beginning of my nine-year journey at Milton Hershey.

When I was accepted to Milton Hershey in the fall of 1960, the day came when I was to take that first 250-mile trip from Butler to my new home. There was a picture of me on the steps of Senior Hall that day. Someone said, "I thought you cried when you went to Hershey, but you are smiling in the picture." That picture was taken before I knew that I was staying and they were going home. I guess I thought we were going to visit a nice place and then we were all going home. But they left me, and the feeling of abandonment—of looking out that upstairs hallway window—had come true again. We went to Cottage Boone, and I was playing in the recreation room with some boys and having fun. When I turned around, Theresa and Chuck were gone. I do not blame them today. I really believe there was no other way to do it. The break had to be quick and unannounced. Nevertheless, I was hurt, angry, and scared. I would have thrown a fit, and my Aunt Theresa was too tenderhearted to bear it. Sometimes, life has to be that way, and it would get worse before it got better. It was like that time I stood at the end of the upstairs hallway and felt that everyone had left me, but this time it was *reality*. Perhaps, you have experienced that kind of loneliness and rejection in your life. It is the place of hopelessness and the center of despair. Although I was not rejected, but rather put there for my own good, I felt rejected. I would have given up if I had known how to do that. I felt trapped, but I had no option except to go forward.

There are many widows that experience this feeling of abandonment at the loss of a life-long mate, or a mother who loses a child, or a sudden divorce that comes out of nowhere, or a little boy who loses his parents. Although all those people mentioned feel abandoned, God is always there, and His plan of destiny moves on in our lives. Cry, cry—like I did for two days and then some! But I beg of you. Let him have His way with you for in the end it is always best. Life is cruel and unfair, but God is a good God! He is good like in *The Touch of the Master's Hand!*

There is a greater lesson in this! God cares, and He is watching. If you turn to Him, He will appear from behind the curtain. It was fifteen years later for me, but He did appear. Every one of us has experienced or will experience this feeling of abandonment and unspeakable loneliness. It is as though our world has ended and there seems to be no sign of hope. This feeling can last a day or years. It is one of those benchmark moments in our lives. In the end, it can be the crossroad that will lead us either to God or to a life of regret, bitterness, and emptiness.

That day, I had no idea what my future held and neither do you. This will not help your hurt, loneliness, or rejection. When there is a dead winter, there can be hope of a springtime and new life if we wait for God. You can make it even when you are sure you cannot. If an eight-year-old boy could *make it* even when he had no idea how, then so can you because God can help you as only God can. God's plans for you are often veiled, but they will not be veiled forever.

CHAPTER 3

My Different Path

These thoughts reveal my journey over the next nine years. I may make spiritual applications at times, but I was not saved in those years. I was not saved until six years after I graduated from high school. The lessons I learned have had a residual effect on me, and after I came to Christ, they became as valuable to me as my perspective on life. Even though the lessons were not spiritual, I love the ways they helped shape my character to deepen my walk with Christ and gave me insight and tools to work with people. God took me from a purposeless life, filled with bitterness and anger toward God because of the death of my parents and the feeling no one wanted me, to a thankfulness and gratefulness that God put this school in my life with my very best interest at heart. My houseparents were Mr. and Mrs. Smith. They were wonderful people full of love and compassion. They helped me with the transition, but my life would change forever. I set sail on a course that would shape my life profoundly. My life had begun at Milton Hershey School.

I learned to work at the orphanage, and I realized I did not like to work. We buffed the kitchen floor with pieces of carpet under our feet. We shuffled and slid and, boy, would that floor shine! I had to make my bed every day and keep my clothes neat. I began to say, "Yes, sir" and "No, ma'am." Not only was it a cultural shock, but I also found out I was lazy. Yes, I had L's disease—laziness. I would receive nine years of this training, and I needed every one of those years. It started my first day. Thankfully, Mr. and Mrs. Smith were nice and patient with me, and I loved them for it. Human beings, for the most part, are naturally lazy. One of the corner stones of Milton Hershey's deed of trust was to teach us the value of work. An honest day's work would bring great success to us later in life. The school's goal was to prepare us for life, but the value of work would be a driving force.

Responsibility and character development was another driving force. I found out that I also lacked character. I will share with you how I failed the test of character, not to exalt my wrongs but rather to teach you what not to do. As in the poem "The Bridge Builder,"

> An old man going a lone highway,
> Came, at the evening cold and gray,
> To a chasm vast and deep and wide.
> Through which was flowing a sullen tide
> The old man crossed in the twilight dim,
> The sullen stream had no fear for him;
> But he turned when safe on the other side
> And built a bridge to span the tide.
>
> "Old man," said a fellow pilgrim near,
> "You are wasting your strength with building here;
> Your journey will end with the ending day,
> You never again will pass this way;
> You've crossed the chasm, deep and wide,
> Why build this bridge at evening tide?"
>
> The builder lifted his old gray head;
> "Good friend, in the path I have come," he said,
> "There followed after me to-day
> A youth whose feet must pass this way.
> This chasm that has been as naught to me
> To that fair-headed youth may a pitfall be;

He, too, must cross in the twilight dim;
Good friend, I am building this bridge for him!"

—By Will Allen Dromgoole
(Source: www.poetryfoundation.org, 2016)
[*Father: An Anthology of Verse*. EP Dutton &
Company, 1931]

I want to build a bridge for you so that you will not have to go through irresponsibility and bad character as I did. The orphanage addressed my weaknesses and helped me grow in my desire to be responsible and have character.

God wants us to be responsible, to have character, and to be holy. He uses tools like the orphanage (the good and the bad), but He also gives us a conscience, as I found out. One night, early into my time in the orphanage, I sneaked out of my bed and into the pantry that every home had. I stole a cookie and slipped away into the dark and back to my bed without getting caught. I did not even leave a crumb to trace. In the morning, when I realized I was not caught, because no one counts the cookies in the cookie jar, I realized that I had a conscience. I could not live with myself, so I turned myself in. It was my first brush with crime. I do not remember what my punishment was. I just remember how it felt to tell the truth and get the guilt off my chest.

What would we be like if we cleared our consciences? A great lesson in the cookie caper! Telling the truth is always best. As you get older, it is harder to cover your cookie crumbs, as I learned much too slowly. Maybe it would be better if we were just like an eight-year-old child whose nature is to do wrong, but who has a conscience to help steer him back on the right path.

I will always be grateful to Milton Hershey School and Milton and Catherine Hershey for what they did for me. As we sang in the Alma Mater, "Thy loyal sons are we then stand we firmly united through the years to come," I grew to have a sense of belonging. Yes,

I am a Hershey boy—a homeboy. Uncle Milt was my father, and this is my story. Today I am forever grateful to God and the opportunity at Milton Hershey.

"A Bag of Tools"

Isn't it strange
That princes and kings,
And clowns that caper
In sawdust rings,
And common people
Like you and me
Are builders for eternity?

Each is given a bag of tools,
A shapeless mass
A book of rules;
And each must make
Ere life is flown
A stumbling block
Or a stepping stone.

—By RL Sharpe
(Source: www.rainydaypoems.com, 2016)

I learned this poem my senior year at Milton Hershey. The poem touched me, but I never understood its depth or the magnitude of its impact on my life. All of life's experiences are woven together like a rug on a loom—each one a thread to be woven. The process is not understood at the time by the rug being woven, but only by the Master Weaver, who chooses each thread carefully.

A Bag of Tools I realized later was Hershey. One of the tools in my bag was opportunity. Milton Hershey gave me the opportunity for an education and access to the wealth that very few have. Milton Hershey left all of his wealth (in the millions) to the school he founded. It was all free, all of it: education, housing, food, clothing, and medical care. Not many get the opportunity that I did, as well as the tools God gave me in my talents, which were hidden when I arrived there at eight years of age.

The "shapeless mass" was the nine years of my journey there and the years thereafter. Time, as in an hourglass, waits for no one. You must use it or lose it. Finally, the "list of rules" was the Bible. I was taught it the whole time I was there, but I did not *get it* until I was twenty-three years old and the book got me. Then I began to realize everything that had happened to me had a purpose. My life went from being a stumbling block to a stepping-stone for me and others. So my journey started when my aunt and uncle dropped me off and ended when I graduated at seventeen years old—the year I learned this poem that fascinated, yet troubled me because I had no idea my life would go from stumbling block to stepping stone.

My Brothers

I was born into a family of three boys. I was the youngest. I was eight years old when my mother died, and my brothers were seven and ten years older than me. Fran was fifteen years old, and Bob was eighteen years old when she died. Bob was named after my father, Robert Maitland. Although I went to Milton Hershey not long after my mother died and was separated from my brothers and did not grow up with them, I still felt close to them and loved them. They have always been special to me, but I can only share a few stories because of our childhood separation.

Bob was not only the oldest and had our father's name, but I felt he was the smartest, best looking, and most congenial. During his senior year, he was voted the most likely to succeed. He loved fast cars and pretty girls. He also had a nose for getting into trouble. At my young age, I was in awe of him because I felt he was *the man*. We were Catholic, and when he got caught stealing hubcaps, the parish priest went to bat for him so that he would not go to jail. Looking back, maybe it would have been the best thing if he had gone to jail. Bob seemed to have a way of getting into trouble, but also of staying ahead of the consequences.

Bob became a printer. He may have studied it in high school. He worked at the local paper *The Butler Eagle*. He was so smooth that he did not get fired for printing the title *Butler Eagle* upside down on the front page. Somehow, he talked his way through it. That was my brother Bob—he was so likeable and so charming.

Bob bought a 1965 Corvette—one of the hottest cars in Butler. The sixties was a decade of muscle cars. It was like "Happy Days," "Arnold's," and "Morgan's Diner." They were the "in" places in Butler. At night, especially on weekends, the muscle cars would show up and circle Morgan's Diner like a car cruise. Bob was in the thick of it in his Corvette, and his reputation grew. Guys would challenge each other on who had the fastest car. They would go somewhere and race, and Bob's reputation grew even more. Even fifty years later I meet people who knew my brother or remembered his car as he had become somewhat of a legend.

He came to see me twice in my nine years at the orphanage. The second time, and the last time I saw him alive, was June 2, 1969. That was the day I graduated from Milton Hershey. Bob came to pick me up and take me home. He came in his '65 Corvette, and it was the first and last time I ever rode in his car. At that point, it was the highlight of my life: I was riding with my cool brother and in his cool car. I could hardly contain myself.

I would not see him again until I saw him after he died. Bob came back to Butler one time after I was married and met my wife; but at that time, I was on Army active duty and did not see him. He was so different from me and my brother, Fran, because he was small in stature and thin like my father. He started drinking just like my father. He traveled the country for the next twenty-five years and ended up in Texas, where he died. All he had left in life were the clothes on his back and a bicycle behind his apartment. When Bob died, he did not have any identification on him so no one knew who he was. They would have buried him in an unmarked grave, and we would have never known he passed away except for a piece of paper he had in his pocket with a phone number on it. Someone called the number, and my brother, Fran, answered the phone. We were able to bring Bob home and bury him next to our parents in Butler. Bob had so many gifts and talents, but he had such a sad ending. Sin and alcohol had stripped him of everything good in life. My heart is still sad when I think of him.

Fran or Francis Maitland was the next oldest. One of the reasons Fran could not apply to Milton Hershey was that the cutoff was age fourteen, and he was one year over the limit. I never knew what it would have been like to have my brother with me in the orphanage. Growing up, Fran and I saw each other from time to time. My brother was a good kid and never got into trouble. Maybe my parents' death hit him the hardest because of his age.

On vacation, I stayed with my Aunt Theresa and Uncle Chuck. Fran stayed with them some, too, until he went into the Navy at age seventeen. It did not go well with Fran at their house. My uncle was a great guy, but a tough one while my brother was not. They clashed. Once, when my brother was stung by a bee, he lay on the ground and screamed. That did not sit well with Uncle Chuck who thought he was being a baby and that a fifteen-year-old should be tougher than that. Fran made me laugh, though, and I loved him.

When he got out of the Navy, Fran married Roxie—a beautiful, but big girl. My brother was six foot five and skinny as a rail.

I said, "Bro, she is a big girl."

He replied, "Dave, the more there is, the more to hug."

They were so happy together. She seemed to keep my brother on the straight and narrow except for his love for cars. He had a 1964 Pontiac LeMans with an overhead cam. He loved to run it until the day he wrapped it around a telephone pole. He was not hurt, but the LeMans was totaled. I felt Fran could have been a racecar driver because he was that good.

When I graduated from the orphanage in 1969, I came to Butler where Fran and Roxie lived. We hung out together for ten years. I had married Bonnie in 1972, and we would go over to their trailer for dinner. We laughed and dreamed. My brother always had a scheme, such as we would open the Maitland Car Wash and become rich. I played along. I loved him so, and I never had a fight with him in all the years we knew each other. Fran was sweetly fickle, and he figured if you thought on it too much, it would drive you crazy. Maybe that is another reason why he and Uncle Chuck did not hit it off. To my uncle, you had to be tough, practical, and save money. My brother was none of those things.

While my brothers drove their Corvette and LeMans, when it was my time to get a car, my uncle bought a 1963 Plymouth Fury with my money, slant six, and push button automatic on the dash. The top end seemed to be thirty-five mph when you went through the push gears. I paid $600 for the car, and I saved money. My uncle was an extremely practical man. He did not want me to waste my money on cars like my brothers had done, so he purchased the car for me. Safe, practical, and economical was his motto. I did not even get a chance to pick it out, but it was mine, and I loved it—even if everyone laughed. Those were the good days with Fran. Then it all changed just like everything else in my life up to that point.

My brother was a brakeman on the B & O Railroad, which came through Butler because it was a steel mill town. My father had worked in the stainless division at Armco Steel Company until he died in 1956. One night, Fran went to work as usual. That night, the workers were short a walkie talkie, so he went into the yard to work among the trains without one. The trains were sitting on the tracks running because they were diesel. They were not to be shut off because that was not cost effective. The train yard was filled with the roar of all the engines— thus the reason for the walkie talkie. My brother's job was to connect and disconnect the cars. While he was disconnecting a car, one of the engines was moved, but he could not tell it was moving because he had his back to that engine. The engine pulled my brother under the train and cut and mangled both of his legs. A few days later, one leg was amputated at the hip, and the other leg was amputated below his knee. It was a gruesome accident with not only the loss of limb, but also the unsanitary conditions of a railroad yard. Infection was inevitable.

I will never forget walking into his hospital room for the first time after the accident. My brother had gone from six foot five to about five feet. It was a shock to see the sheets flat to the bed where his legs should be. It was a hard sight to see. His life was never the same. That day, I had the joy of leading Fran to Christ. I had just become a Christian a few years before. How sad to see his broken body, but oh, the joy that Fran's soul would go to heaven someday!

Roxie was a great wife. She not only stayed with my brother, but also loved him and nursed him back from death's door. There were many painful operations. I admired Fran so much because the boy of fifteen that my uncle thought was a baby for crying over a bee sting showed amazing courage and manhood in dealing with his pain. I am not sure I could have been as strong and courageous as my brother was.

To make the tragedy even sadder, after Fran was stabilized, he had to begin to learn to live without his legs, which was so hard for me to see. This six foot five strapping guy was reduced to a wheelchair and various skin grafts, bedsores, infections, and surgeries. Just as things were looking up, Roxie seemed to get a bad case of the flu and went into the hospital for tests. She had labored so hard to care for my brother that we all thought she had worn herself out and gotten sick. They admitted Roxie and within twenty-four hours, she was dead. She had acute leukemia and did not know it. We were all shocked. Fran had lost the love of his life. We left Meadville where we lived at the time to come for the viewing and funeral, thinking we would be returning with Fran's two children, Sherry and Todd, as Fran was still mostly bedridden. However, he surprised us all by being up in his wheelchair and asking to learn simple things to cook, determined his children would remain with him.

Fran remarried shortly after and spent the next twenty years as a hermit. Although we called and stayed close at heart, we did not see each other much. His new wife wanted it that way, and I wanted to make it easy for him. We loved each other and never had cross words between us. How sad his life became, but I will fellowship with him in heaven because of his faith and trust in Christ. I cherish my memories of him for he passed away several years ago.

I am now brotherless. I am blessed and have reconciled the loss of my brothers, but I loved them both. God had a different plan for me. I often say, "Why me, Lord?" Why would God love me so much to do what He has done for me? I am forever grateful for my life. I found out years later that my mother, who had become a Christian, prayed for me that I would be a preacher. That is what I am today. I pray I will be faithful in His service until He comes for me in the rapture or calls me home.

My favorite book of the Bible is the book of Ruth. I am a romantic, and I never lose the thrill of this widowed woman who seemed to have lost everything and appeared to be abandoned in life. As you read the book, you will see the destiny of Ruth unfold without God speaking a word in the book. But He is there everywhere in the book of Ruth, working His will from start to finish. I learned that there is nothing more visible in life than an invisible God. From Moab to the Messianic line. Who knew? Only God. I believe He is working behind the scenes in your life if you are willing to wait and see what that is. It is so sad that Orpah did not. I know that He was especially working in the life of an eight-year-old boy named David Hilary Maitland.

Maybe that is why everyone passed on me. My middle name was "Hilary." Just joking. Who has a middle name like Hilary? Seriously. That is like "A Boy Named Sue." I love my first name, David, which means beloved, and I am honored by the name Maitland. But Hilary? What's up with that? To put a boy in a 1,500-boy orphanage with a middle name of Hilary is deadly. That's a girl's name. Let me tell you that I hid it for all nine years and was successful until the day I graduated. In a graduating class of 168, they messed up my name and had to read it twice. David Hilary Maitland. How embarrassing! My only consolation was that it was my last day at the school. Once again, God has a plan in everything.

One day after I graduated, someone explained to me why my middle name was Hilary. I don't know if it is true or not, but one of my family members told me that my mother named me after Sir Edmund Hillary who attempted to climb Mt. Everest in 1952, the year I was born. My mother not only had the guts to name me Hilary, but I believe she had great aspiration for me in my life. My mother had me when she was forty-two years old, and even though I only had her for eight years, I still feel a special bond between us. I now cherish my middle name and am honored that my middle name is Hilary. I love my name, David Hilary Maitland. It seems so complete now.

"You don't have to be a fantastic hero to do certain things—to compete. You can be just an ordinary chap, sufficiently motivated to reach challenging goals. The intense effort, the giving of everything you've got, is a very pleasant bonus."

Sir Edmund Hillary

CHAPTER 4

Milton Hershey School—The Main—Learning Whom to Trust

My fourth through sixth grade years were spent in the Main Division or as we called it "The Main." It seemed to be my first real contact with life. I learned that I liked sports, although I had seldom played. I began to play baseball and basketball. Even though I did not know much about these sports, I seemed to have somewhat of a knack for them. Sports were a big part of Milton Hershey, and they became a big part of my life. Sports helped to build the character traits of toughness, discipline, and teamwork that fit into the Hershey ideal. In a school of 1,500 boys, it is hard to get noticed, and you become a face in the crowd. I saw sports as a way to get noticed and to be accepted. I was small, shy, and young for my grade, but I had finally found a way to be accepted. I wanted to do something I was good at.

God gives us the desire to accomplish, to excel, and to become our best at something. For some at the orphanage, it was not sports, but rather choir, band, studies, drama, or student council. All of these were offered by the school to give us avenues to succeed. When we failed, it would crush our dreams or reveal how that area may not be our area of talent. It is important then to search for another talent, which causes us to try harder or dig deeper to bring out that God-given talent. We may switch areas, but we must not give up. We must understand why we are trying to succeed and gain the approval of our peers.

I so wanted to be accepted. I felt there was some way I could gain this respect. It did not matter if it was a *corruptible* crown ...I just wanted to be crowned. I later learned in my life that there was an *incorruptible crown* and that my efforts to succeed and excel were to glorify God, which gave me great satisfaction. There is a spot that God has carved out for you. It may not be what your parents dreamed for you or even what you dreamed for yourself. We are crushed sometimes by the expectations of others and ourselves. You should always examine your options—EYO I've learned to call it. But God has plans for you if you will let Him help you. "For I know the thoughts that I think toward you, saith the Lord, thoughts of peace, and not of evil, to give you an expected end" (Jer. 29:11). Milton Hershey opened me up to the world of sports and gave me a great tool for my tool box for later in life.

Even with a broken heart, the orphanage began to expose me to life and to teach me many lessons that would stay with me for life. When I went there, I had no idea who Milton Hershey was, why he died, what he did, or who owned this place where I lived. I was given everything I needed like new clothes, new suits, new shirts, and new shoes. It was fun to go to the clothing center and pick out new things, but I had no idea who paid for them or why I was getting them. There was the new food. Some tasted good, but some tasted not so good. One of the things that did not taste so good was chow chow, a pickled medley of vegetables. I still enjoy the taste of Shepherd's pie. All of it was nutritious, well-balanced, and part of the plan. Imagine what a monster challenge it was to send out daily food to 1,500 boys scattered in home settings all over Hershey.

I did not realize or appreciate it at the time until years after I had left the school that I was placed into a wealthy, organized, purpose-driven, elite family created with my future in mind so that I could succeed in life. Two things blocked my understanding of what a gift I was given. The first was the loneliness and rejection of losing my parents and being taken from my family surroundings. These feelings kept me from appreciating what was being done for me in the grand way. It is not the abundance of things we get that make us happy but rather our perspective on life. In many cases at the home, the rejection was replaced with bitterness and ungratefulness.

The second block was even though the plan and the wealth was great, not everyone in the plan was kind. Their human nature took over. Some leadership did not have the heart for the kids. They were few, but they were there. Also, when you put 1,500 boys together, there was bound to be conflict, bullying, fighting, and some level of meanness. The school tried hard to prevent this, so this is not a criticism of the school overall.

Mr. Hershey died in 1945, but when he was alive, he knew that he could not be everywhere. He tried to make his school the best. He knew that each boy needed to learn how to succeed in this life. Eventually his plan worked, our broken hearts healed, and we would become men. We became the men of Milton Hershey. He knew that the loneliness, rejection, and unfairness of life could be overcome because of all the things he had overcome. He wanted us to struggle for it, that was the discipline part, and not just have it handed to us. I remember three struggles I learned from when I was at the Main or Elementary Division.

Watch Whom You Trust

The first struggle was that not every creature in life is friendly. For some reason a couple of us started to chase a chipmunk. It looked so cute, and I thought it would make a nice pet. You may ask, "How could you be fast enough to catch a chipmunk?" I was not fast enough out in the open yard, but when it jumped into a window well at ground level, I went after it and caught it. For a second, I looked him right in the face with sheer joy. And I mean *a second*, for I have never been bitten so hard in all my life. Wow, did that hurt! I immediately let him go and realized that he was not my friend. I was not going to hurt him. I just wanted a pet, but I learned that not every creature on earth wanted to be my friend. I have never tried to pick up a chipmunk again, and I suggest the same to you. Not everything in life is your friend. Be careful what you pick up.

The second struggle I learned from was that not everyone in life is going to be your friend. Somewhere around the fifth grade I made a kid mad. His name was Ben Riggin, and I do not know what I did or why he was so angry. I *do* know he was the toughest kid in the whole Main Division. This was the early sixties, and he looked like Fonzi with brown hair. He told me to meet him at the flagpole the next day after lunch. I could hardly sleep because I knew that he would beat the daylights out of me. If you saw how small and scrawny I was, you would have agreed. I am not sure why, but I showed up. Fortunately, he did not show up, and I lived to write this today. He never mentioned it again and neither did I. That is when I realized that not every human being is your friend and life could become cruel at any given moment.

Life is sometimes filled with people who want to pick a fight. This frightened me and was my first experience with "the pecking order." Everyone has his or her place in it, and you better learn when to open your mouth and when to close it or someone will do it for you. I also learned what is really worth fighting for. It can be a cruel world. I learned I could make it alone. Friends are good, but one day I learned "if God be for us, who can be against us" (Rom. 8:31). You may have a Ben Riggin in your life sometime, along with good friendships like the kind I had with Jerry Doyle and Jimmy McCauley. The strong bond with these home boys was one of the reasons I became such a loyalist. The bad situations with people are scary, and the good ones cause you to cherish and appreciate them.

The third lesson that I learned at the Main in my elementary years was that you cannot trust everyone in life even if they seem to have good intentions. It is your responsibility to figure out if they are trustworthy. We were in gym class, and, like everything else, Hershey gave us a well-rounded experience, even in gym. I did not like rope climbing in class because at that time in my life I had zero upper body strength, but they made me try. I finally got to the top, but it was so hard. We did other things like swimming, which was great except for one reason—I could not swim. No one had ever taught me to swim, even though on my mom's side of the family two of my cousins were all-American swimmers. Class went well. I stayed in the shallow end while Mr. Morgan, our teacher, kept an eye on us. I can tell you specifically that it was the class right before lunch, and we had spaghetti that day… No, you just do not forget days like this.

Some boys got out of the pool and began to change. Mr. Morgan was sitting just outside the pool door watching those in the pool and those who went to the locker room to change. For some reason, one of my newfound friends and I lingered by the pool. He said to me, "Let's jump in the deep end."

I said, "I can't swim yet."

He said, "It's easy. Just jump in and paddle your arms and legs, and you will be fine. If you start to go under, I will jump in and help you."

That sounded good to me! So I did! Immediately, I did what he said and immediately I kept going under. So Plan B was he would jump in and save me! That sounded good, too, but it did not work. I panicked and began to drown. He panicked and swam to safety. After bobbing and hollering, I felt like on the third time I was going down for good. That final time I saw Mr. Morgan turn. He caught my eye as I was going down. He dove in like Tarzan, swam the length of the pool, swooped me out of the water, and placed me on the side of the pool. Thank you, Mr. Morgan. I am writing this because you were a trustworthy gym teacher. My buddy and I stayed friends, lunch was good and memorable, and I did learn to swim; however, I was a lot more careful about whom I trusted when I was encouraged to do something.

Always watch whom you trust. It could make you or break you in life. It almost broke me. People mean well, but make sure they are people who can live up to what they are saying. Others just want to lead you astray, and in those cases you will get caught holding the bag. They will be long gone. Others are just plain stupid or *simple* as the Bible calls it. They lack common sense. If you follow them, you will drown in life for sure. I learned how to pray about things, and to test people by spirit and deed first, before I leaped.

Somewhere during my years at the Main I met Jimmy McCauley, who would become my best friend in the school for the whole time I was there. Good friends are hard to find in life, and I have been blessed with probably more than the average. Some friendships come together by circumstances, such as Jimmy and me because we were both orphans and great friends all through our experience at Hershey. However, it was during my junior high and senior high years that Jimmy and I were the closest.

CHAPTER 5

Intermediate Division—
The Disciplined Life

The 1,500 boys at Milton Hershey were broken down by homes into three divisions, the elementary or the main division, the intermediate division of sixth through eighth grades, and the senior division of ninth through twelfth grades with each home having fourteen to thirty boys. As I moved into my intermediate division years, I was placed into a new student home with new houseparents and a new group of about fourteen boys. It was like starting all over again. The home was even brand new. Steigel was the name of a new home, which was named after a local man who became famous for Stiegel Glassworks in Manheim, Pennsylvania, Lancaster County.

My new houseparents were Mr. and Mrs. Aikens. They were different from the Smiths of my junior experience at the Main. The Aikens were great people who loved kids, loved their job, and were good houseparents, but they were tough, practical, and fair. I did not appreciate them as much until years later. Maybe that was because of the new kids I befriended during my intermediate time—Joe, Jake Pazzuli, Steve Castleberry, and others. I began to get a chip on my shoulder. I wanted to get out of the school. Jake and Joe were able to talk their families into getting them out. Steve and I were not so lucky, or so we thought.

It was the beginning of some tough times. As I began to mature physically, I found out how much I enjoyed sports, but I could not seem to get into the regimen of the discipline of everyday life at my student home, Steigel. We were to be up early doing chores and having a set study time, shower time, and bedtime. Pretty much the same every night, day after day, and year after year! Maybe that is why I hate hellos and goodbyes. I seem to like the middle of relationships more. This was all new again. I had a new house, new friends, and new houseparents who were bound and determined to make a disciplined man out of me or at least start the process properly. It is hard to start from scratch with new surroundings and the fear of acceptance with new friends. I was painfully shy and the pecking order was a killer. You lead, get in line, or get stepped on. I decided to get in line and that would get me into trouble.

This is the age where peer pressure begins to rear its head. The best way to describe my rebelliousness was labor vs. management. We were the labor, and the school was management. I saw it as hard labor forced upon me by the school. The school was doing it for my benefit, but I began to resent it as I was influenced by my peers. It is almost like Charles Dickens's *Oliver Twist* portrayed with the exception that my surroundings were wonderful and lavish because of the kindness of the chocolate magnet Milton Hershey. I still had the influence of the *artful dodgers* of this world. It is hard for people to imagine, but even in a world in which you have the best of everything provided for you, some can be ungrateful and unhappy and work against the very system that is trying to help them. When people are given things, they will be ungrateful unless they are taught to appreciate those things. Milton Hershey had thought of that, too. It is not money that changes character. In these years, I did not know it, but I was entering into Character Class 101. These would be hard years of my life, especially my senior high school years.

I wanted to get out of Milton Hershey many times. My Uncle Chuck made me stay, and the school worked on my character. I am grateful today to both my uncle and my precious alma mater, Milton Hershey.

Home Life

The Stiegel home housed up to fourteen boys with an apartment for the houseparents and another small apartment for weekend help. It was set on three to five acres. We had no grass when we moved in. When we got in trouble, we would have to pick up rocks in the yard so that the grass would grow. Mr. Aikens was a wise man. If we did something wrong, instead of yelling, he would give us a bucket, and we would have to pick up rocks. I guess you could say I picked a few in my day. Mostly it was for not learning to make my bed, for too many demerits, for not doing my chores right, or for disobedience. A bucket of rocks here, a bucket of rocks there—Character 101. Eventually, we had grass and no more rocks. Great! Then I learned about a flower called the dandelion. At Hershey, our grass had to be a beautiful lush green, which is why we picked up the rocks. But now that we had grass, we picked buckets of dandelions. We could not pluck the head off. We used a special fork to dig them up by the roots. A kid could do a lot of thinking when he was digging dandelions. I learned to keep my bed neat, and I was careful not to get too many demerits. I have to say that, in the long run, it worked.

Demerits

I experienced the demerit system for the first time in the Intermediate Division when I entered the sixth grade and moved to my new student home, Keystone Steigel. Steigel was the home within the Keystone cluster and, therefore, easy to find. There may have been around one hundred homes at the school with so many boys to train.

We had a clipboard with twenty or more tasks we had to do daily. The tasks included: making your bed properly, barn work, doing dishes, cleaning, outside work, collecting trash, and promptness to meals and to the limo when it pulled out for school. If you failed in any area, you would get ten demerits or more if they felt the offense deserved them. Each week the demerits were tallied up. If we went over a certain amount, we suffered a loss of privileges or were given extra work like picking up rocks and digging dandelions. Once a week, when we became old enough, we would go to town on what was called *town privilege*. That was the toughest privilege to lose. It meant so much to go into town once a week to see a movie or just to see real people "on the outside." Town privilege was highly restricted, but it was our only hope to see the outside world. And you had to be on time when the limo arrived to take you back to the unit.

The demerit system was a tough system because it monitored most of my everyday life. As I look back now, it helped me to learn personal discipline—something I desperately needed. The best way to form good habits is to learn them day in and day out. The monotony of discipline year after year becomes part of the fabric of your life. For example: I had to say "yes ma'am," "no ma'am," "yes, sir," and "no sir," or I would get demerits. I still do that today even when people tell me not to. I learned one major lesson from the demerit system: fulfilling your responsibility results in privileges. Responsibilities equal privileges. If I did not complete the responsibility on the daily worksheet, I did not get the privilege I wanted. The lowest form of motivation is punishment for which the demerit system was an effective tool. I would later learn that there are other forms of motivation.

Motivation
_____ Love—the highest form of motivation
_____ Honor
_____ Duty
_____ Reward

Punishment

The discipline system can be flawed by the person in charge. I will admit that I felt demerits were given at times when someone just wanted to make my life miserable. Even those demerits in the end made me stronger because I also learned that life is not always fair and that systems may have flaws. It stands to reason because we are flawed human beings. At every one of these levels of motivation, I believe that fulfilled responsibility equals privilege, and that works out in the end whether life or the system is fair or not.

During many of my years at the school, I chaffed under the demerit and discipline system and often became bitter. God knew that I needed to become responsible, and He allowed me to be shaped by this rigid system as well as in other ways. I think this is what Milton Hershey meant for us to learn about life. He loved his parents, but saw his father as a shiftless dreamer with no responsibility about him and his mother as a rigid disciplinarian.

Milton Hershey was trying to make men out of boys, orphan boys, so that they could make it in this tough world. In our alma mater song, we have a line that says, "We're men of Milton Hershey." God knew I needed that discipline. It goes beyond the demerit system. Discipline was in every aspect of my life at Hershey—in the home, in the classroom, and in the wrestling room. Hebrews 12:11a says, "Now no chastening for the present seemeth to be joyous." I was not joyous at the time I experienced these things, but God knew I needed this discipline to eventually make me a godly man.

Fights

I experienced my first fights in the Intermediate Division. It was a natural part of an all-boys school, and sooner or later there would be some fights. It is maybe a little comical, but my first fight was scheduled by my houseparent, Mr. Aikens. One of the guys in the home and I must have been arguing about something. Mr. Aikens said he had enough. He made us put on boxing gloves and go downstairs to the wrestling mat and slug it out. I do not remember much, but I *do* remember it was the first time I realized that I had a left hook, being a south paw that I am. When we were done, we shook hands and were friends again.

I had another fight in junior high when I was at Steigel, but I had forgotten about it until a few years ago. When I finished praying at our alumni banquet forty years later, a man who was in Steigel with me came to me and said, "Dave, you have to come and meet my wife."

He introduced her to me and said, "This is Dave Maitland. When we were kids in the home, I was snapping Dave with a towel, and Dave said, 'If you do that one more time I am going to punch you in the eye.' I snapped him again, and he punched me in the eye just like he said he would. He threatened that he would do it again if I told on him."

He was so proud of that story, and we laughed. I felt terrible, and I apologized. To him, it was the wonderful mystic of the home, the good old days.

I never liked fights and still do not today. I have found there are no winners in most of them. I always felt bad hurting the other person's feelings, and if I lost, I was hurt.

Dishes

I learned to do dishes in the orphanage sometimes because it was part of my chores and sometimes as a punishment. I have had dishpan hands so many times I cannot count. There were fourteen boys to a unit plus houseparents, resulting in a lot of dishes to do. It taught me teamwork and the assembly-line mentality that I still have today. Doing dishes is all about rhythm. You get the food from the table, scrape and stack the dishes, wash, rinse, and dry the dishes, and put them away. We worked in crews, and after a while you would get a rhythm. It helped everyone work better, and the job got done faster. But oh! Those pots and pans were the dirtiest job in the kitchen. I used to dread it. We washed and polished those big aluminum pans with Brillo pads until they shone. The houseparents would inspect them before we could be dismissed. It was hard work, but I learned how to scrub pots and pans. While it may seem unrelated, I also learned not to waste food because of my pots and pans experience. We rarely saved the food if it was left over because the meal truck would come for the next meal and bring more food. It was hard to estimate so there was a lot of waste. Before I scrubbed and polished the pans, I had to dump out the food, and it would bother me to waste food. I tried to always clean my plate—even today—for two reasons: I saw all the waste when I cleaned those pots and pans, and when I put food on my plate, I had to eat it or else I would get demerits. I had to take a little of everything—even things like succotash, beets, and chow chow.

Sports

It was during this time in my life that I discovered I liked sports and seemed to have a little knack for it. My brothers never got into sports in any way, but for me it opened a whole new world. Because there were so many boys in the school, intramural sports between units was a big deal. We had soccer, baseball, and a lot of pick-up basketball games. In the sixth grade, they even had a novice-wrestling tournament. I would have loved to play football, but I was a late bloomer and too small. We never had golf at the school so that was out. I did pitch one game in our intramural league, but when I threw a pitch and it went over the backstop, my career was short-lived.

My best friend, Jimmy McCauley, talked me into the sixth grade novice wrestling tournament. It is mostly a blur. The one thing

I *do* remember was that I somehow ended up wrestling Jimmy. He beat me 14-2, and the only reason I had two points was because he let me up just to take me down again. It was a flat-out massacre, but Jimmy was my friend so I did not mind. I truly was the poster child for a sixty-five-pound weakling. The strangest thing happened after the match with Jimmy. It was one of those times when destiny stepped in.

The varsity wrestling coach, Don Witman, came up to me, put his arm around me, and said, "Dave, someday you are going to be a great wrestler."

I figured he was lying through his teeth, but it was the first time I felt someone believed in me. That day I changed on the inside, and that memory would come back later to play a big part in my life.

In junior high, I found that I had a great love for basketball, as we would play all the time at Steigel. It was in the days of Jerry West and Peter Marovich—they were our heroes. We loved to play one-on-one or two-on-two, and we would even go out and shovel the snow off the court in the winter so that we could play. While I never played on our high school team, being five foot two and eighty-five pounds in ninth grade, watching and playing basketball all those years gave me a great understanding of the game and was valuable later when I coached basketball for twenty years.

Sports became part of the fabric of my life; and not only built both my body and the discipline that comes with sports through commitment, but also hard work, teamwork, and a sense of Esprit de corps. It started in these early years and carried through my high school years and throughout my life. When I became a Christian years later, I used sports to build Christ-like character in the players I coached.

I missed other sports like hunting and golf because the orphanage did not offer these. They were not going to let 1,500 orphans have rifles. My grandson, Sawyer, enjoys hunting and trapping. I go with him, but my knowledge of these areas is limited. Although I am willing to go, he knows I am too much of a softie to kill anything.

He loves to tease me. Once when I was hunting, I came face to face with a mink. When we looked each other in the eye, I felt badly for him so I shooed him away. Once, I caught some fish at my father-in-law's hunting camp. I put them in the sink to revive them, and then threw them back in the creek. I always blame it on the orphanage because they took that part of my life away. I think it is just me, but I love hanging out with my grandson so I play along. He sees right through me though.

Vacations

The school allowed me to go on vacation three times a year if I had a place to go. Some boys stayed at "The Home" all year round because they did not have any family or what family they had could not keep them. I was fortunate in that area because my Aunt Theresa and Uncle Chuck always said I could stay with them. We were allowed one week at Christmas, one week at Easter, and one month in the summer. That was it. I cherished every one of them.

It was from this part of my life at Hershey that I realized what an emotional person I was. I am a romantic, idealist, and a purist—all rolled into one. I found myself all wrapped up in these vacation times. On my first trip home for Christmas at eight-years-old, I was so small my feet did not touch the floor of the Greyhound bus when I was sitting. I had to have an older boy from the home with me. Perry Dawson from Butler would go with me so I would not get lost. We took a van seven miles to Harrisburg, then boarded a Greyhound bus to travel 250 miles on the Turnpike to Pittsburgh, and then got transferred to another Greyhound bus for thirty-five miles to Butler. My family would pick me up at the bus station. It was an all-day process. Hershey had a way of forging friendships for life. Over fifty years later, Perry Dawson and I live in the same area of Butler, Pennsylvania. Perry is a retired business teacher of Knoch High School, and I am a pastor. A long way past being eight-year-old boys on a bus, we are bound together by the orphanage where we spent so many years together.

I lived for vacations. I counted the months and days in advance to each one with my anticipation growing. I could hardly sleep the night before I left for Butler. I savored every moment of the trip and the experience home. I never tired of the wonder of it. My first few days home were filled with the ecstatic joy of being somewhere I felt loved. I counted the days carefully every day and enjoyed every moment with my friends and family. I believe this is where I became a lover of life and how I came to appreciate life in individually small chunks. Life is extremely precious. Around midway through my vacation, the feelings of dread would begin to come, even as I tried to fight them off and savor the moment. The day of dread arrived, and I had to board the bus and head back to school. I shed tears when I was younger and felt bitterness and regret when I was older. The ride back to Hershey was always terrible and depressing. This process went on for the nine years that I was at the orphanage. I learned to love and dread the smell of the bus diesel fuel. I loved it on the way home and dreaded it on the way back to school.

These moments of my life are etched in my memory. I learned all good things come to an end so I better enjoy the time between the hellos and goodbyes. I want to love and to be loved and live with expectancy that life could end tomorrow. I am a lover not a fighter because life is too short. These trips reminded me of that truth three times a year. In my life, the Lord has made this desire to cherish life even stronger. We fight over the silliest things. I did not want to fight, but rather belong somewhere, belong to someone, and have a vacation that would never end. I wanted a family of my own and to be crazy in love with my wife, my children, and my Lord since I have been saved. You say I could not have gotten that from just a bus trip. Yes, I did. You had to experience it to understand it. Those trips were joys of ecstasy, happiness, pain, sorrow, and rejection when I could not stay. That is life, and everyone deals with it differently.

Rhythm of a Disciplined Life

Back at the home at Milton Hershey, my life at Steigel was safe. My houseparents were fair and strict. My junior high years began to take on a rhythm. My rhythm was as follows: get up early, do chores, go to school, come back home from school, eat supper, play, study, shower, go to bed, and go to church every Sunday. There was minimal change in those nine years. At that time I called it boring and monotonous; but today, I would call it the rhythm of a disciplined life. The school was great for that. There was a certain part of my character that desperately needed that discipline, although I did not know it at the time. It was not necessarily spiritual, but it was building the frame of my character like the steel beams of a building. They cannot be seen, but they are there holding up the building. Milton Hershey knew we needed that. Although we had every luxury life could give, we had to work every day and stay on this rigid schedule.

The ability to work hard and be consistent is a great discipline in life. That did not come naturally for me, but nine years at Milton Hershey pointed me in the right direction. It starts with the little things in life. I had to be up on time, make my bed, be respectful, do my homework, shower every day, follow the rules, clean my plate, and the list goes on. In sports they call it doing the basics, and from that you can do great things in life, such as get a job, pay your bills, provide for your family, and do well in your chosen career. While it sounds crazy, it works, and it worked for Milton S. Hershey in his life. He passed that on to me and thousands of other boys and girls through the years, even though I did not appreciate it at the time.

Another part of Hershey was the friends I made. My friendships began to take shape in my junior high years between sixth and eighth grade. They grew stronger and deeper in my senior high years between ninth and twelfth grade. I struggled with one aspect of these relationships. In a school like Milton Hershey, kids would come and go. I was always meeting new kids, and some of them would not stay. Most of us wanted to get out of the school, and some did. Some, who were my friends, such as Jake Pazzuli, talked their families into letting them get out. It was so hard on me. I became close to Jake and other guys, but they left like Jake did in junior high. It left a big hole in my life, and sometimes that hole was hard to fill. I wanted out, but there was no chance of me getting out. It was not the school's fault. I was so far from home and felt lonely and wanted to be with family. Today, I am so glad I stayed and graduated from Milton Hershey. I never saw guys like Jake again. I wonder where he is today and what his life came to be.

My life began to take on some unusual paradoxes. The steady discipline of the school gave me a stable foundation to live every day by getting up, grinding life out, and being consistent by doing the simple daily tasks of life. Discipline and a strong work ethic were part of Milton Hershey's success in his life. On the other hand, there was instability brought on by being an orphan. Your orphan family increased or decreased on a monthly or yearly basis with Jake Pazzuli and others leaving. Sometimes you would just get to know someone, and they would leave. Also, after I went home for vacation, I had to come back, and the readjustment would start again. A stable and yet an unstable world that I lived in shaped my outlook on life in many ways. Everything was the same day after day; and yet, in these other ways my surroundings or those who surrounded me could change any minute. This left me with a strange insecurity.

When I went back to the orphanage this past year, I went into the choir room and there were 135 choir members—all part of the Milton Hershey student body. There were boy and girl partial orphans, full orphans, and social orphans of all races and creeds. I walked into the room and in less than a minute I bonded with most, if not all, of them. I looked into their eyes, they looked into mine, and we understood each other. It was the same look I had when I was in the school, which said I longed to be loved. We want to be loved, and we can spot someone who can understand our heart. The look said, "Will you love me?" and yet held a trace of fear that said, "Will you leave me as others did?" and we clicked. We were strong in what we learned, yet vulnerable because of the circumstances that made us a part of the school. There was a bond between us that day.

Before I prayed for these students, I blurted out, "I should bring you all a candy bar next year."

The room went up in a roar.

I walked out and said to my wife, "I just committed myself to 135 candy bars next year. I love it!"

They stole my heart in one minute. Their eyes said, "Will you love me?" They saw in my eyes that I am one of them. I have been where they are now. I understand, and I will love them. In Matthew 9:36, Jesus had compassion because they were like sheep without a shepherd. He understood their hearts.

If you have had an experience like the orphanage, I believe you can spot a lonely heart longing to belong, longing to be loved. Sad to say, this longing can be filled in the wrong way in shallow relationships, career gratification, or a life of empty dreams. I have experienced this loneliness, this longing which can become all-consuming, and I seem to be able to spot it in people. I have a burden to help people in this state to find real joy, peace, and purpose in life like others who helped me along the way. Milton Hershey School gave us all the tools we need to be successful in life whether or not graduates want to admit it. It is the heart of a person that will use these tools for a stumbling block or a stepping stone. Loneliness can only be settled in the heart. By the end of this book, I hope you will understand that. When I left that choir room, the students did not steal 135 candy bars from me, but rather they stole my heart. That is what breathes life and hope into the tools we have. "Keep thy heart with all diligence; for out of it are the issues of life" (Prov. 4:23).

CHAPTER 6

Senior High Years—Life is Not Always Fair

Lest you think I am pompously spiritual, I am not. My heart has not always been this way. As I moved into my senior high years at the orphanage, I experienced my most troubling times at Milton Hershey. I do not blame Milton Hershey at all for without his dream and generosity my life would be different, and everyone else who went to the school would probably have not had a better life. The MHS deed of trust, for all of us that made it through the school, is a precious mission statement—a testimony to Milton Hershey for his vision in many ways of knowing what unfortunate children like us needed to survive. But one can find fault with the human implementation of that mission statement if they want. We still fight over the meaning of the deed of trust today. Milton Hershey School is a great school even with its human flaws one hundred years later.

Even with all the unfairness of life I experienced at MHS, especially in my high school years, it was all part of the plan and helped to build character, which I would need for the rest of my life. I might add that I share my imperfections in these next chapters because I was no angel. I was a bitter orphan looking for someone to love me, and it was my character that needed to be shaped. Sometimes, there was joy; and other times, there was pain. I am going to let you in on my sometimes turbulent years—not embellishing my character or the school's but being painfully honest. I love Milton Hershey School and will stand by it for what it did in my life by God's direction. "All hail to thee Milton Hershey; thy loyal sons are we." It was living through it that was tough at the time. Life can be also.

In the 1960s, Milton Hershey was going through a building boom. They built clusters of new homes—probably hundreds of them—and downsized the thirty boys in a home to fifteen boys in a home. The homes were new and beautiful. I believe it was around 1962 that I went to the new student home, Steigel, for my junior high years. In 1965, I moved into the senior division, starting my high school years at another brand new home called Rock Ridge. We were never allowed to refer to our houseparents by their first names. It was yes ma'am, no ma'am, yes sir, and no sir. Our houseparents were probably both in their fifties. They both smoked, and they were tough. Everything was by the book as they saw it. I do not remember any warm and fuzzy times. To be honest, in my eyes, they could be extremely unkind if they wanted to be, and you learned quickly not to cross them. Many a boy came to our home and tried to transfer to another home. Some were successful and some were not. Rick Zilmer was able to move after two years to another unit, but I stayed at Rock Ridge all four years until I graduated from Milton Hershey. Rick later became a four-star general in the Marines, and when we got together some forty years later, we talked about our years at Rock Ridge.

In my mind, my high school years were tough, yet rewarding in many ways. They helped to build the character lessons I would draw upon the rest of my life. The best way for me to explain this is not in a chronological order but rather by the different aspects the school provided: home life (my time spent at Rock Ridge), sports, my school life at the famous school on the hill that you can see from Hershey Park called Senior Hall, music of the 60s that deeply affected me, my religious experience, and relationships. Lessons I learned about life in an institutionalized setting made up of homes caring for 1,500 boys from all over the country proved invaluable. To me, it became the best institution I could have been in, and I am intensely grateful and loyal to it. MHS was like family to me. I can say things about it, but you better not. We became a kind of band of brothers. To us Milton Hershey School was a world unto itself—sometimes far removed from the outside world.

The Home—Rock Ridge

I was at Rock Ridge for my ninth through twelfth grade years. There were fourteen boys to a home with two boys to a bedroom. Our wake-up time was 5:45 every day. All the lights in the boys' wing were turned on with one switch, so when 5:45 a.m. came, all the lights came on with a seeming thud. And if you did not get up, the housefather would come and get you out of bed. Why 5:45? The homes in our senior high cluster had about thirty cows in a barn that had to be milked. The barn chores and house chores had to be done before breakfast and school. Sometimes, my chores would be putting feed in the young calves' pen, feeding silage to the cows, or washing the cow's tails with a bucket of hot soapy water with cocoa butter bars left over from the Hotel Hershey. Our cows had the smoothest, cleanest tails ever. There was an art form to snapping them dry like cracking a whip. We had electric milkers, and we would keep charts every day on each cow of how much they gave. Since 5:45 a.m. was early, sometimes I would fall asleep when I was milking with my head braced up against the cow's leg so I would not get kicked because sometimes a cow would get touchy. One day when I was milking, I fell asleep and was rudely awakened by a cow's tail that had been just washed, slapping right across my face.

I liked barn chores better than house chores. The cows had to be milked twice a day. The school could have brought in two dairy men to work the barn, but they used about fifteen boys in the cluster around the barn to do it. We would rotate in our home every week or two so that we could all have that experience. It was the Hershey way to teach us character and expose us to every aspect they could expose us to while we were growing up. I have a deep appreciation for the farm today and never complain when milk prices go up because I know what it takes for a farmer to get a gallon of milk.

I remember walking to the barn those one hundred yards in the winter when the wind was blowing and I had just jumped out of bed. As I got older and was wrestling at ninety-eight pounds, the wind would cut like a knife and almost blow me over. Just getting to the barn seemed to be a great accomplishment. I never milked cows nor did barn work after those four years at MHS, but it gave me a great appreciation for farmers in what they do and how hard they work. In this book, you will hear me say a number of times that I learned the value of hard work during my years working in the barns.

If I was not doing barn work, I was learning the value of hard work by doing house chores at Rock Ridge. Beds were made, and we had a list of chores to do every day. Each month the students would rotate so we would experience the full spectrum of washing and drying dishes, scrubbing pots and pans, setting and clearing tables for mealtime, sweeping and scrubbing floors, and keeping the home spotless every day. You never knew when someone might stop by unannounced. If we knew someone important was coming or it was a special weekend like Mother's Day, we would put some extra spit and polish on the whole home. We had the best curb appeal in the whole world.

The Giggle

I learned to eat fast and get my work done, or I would get extra chores. That is probably why I eat quickly to this day. There were things to do and no time to dawdle. I do remember a time when our table of guys started giggling about something. We heard the command to stop giggling from our houseparent. We tried, but it is hard to shut that spigot off when it starts flowing. Then we heard that the next person who laughs will do all the dishes and pans for everyone's meal. Do you want to take a guess who could not help themselves and let out a chuckle? You guessed it. Me. I ended up doing all the dishes and pans. For some reason things like this hit me hard. I was angry, bitter, and alone, and no one was allowed to help me. I guess that is the way life is sometimes.

The White Glove

One day, I had the chore to clean and dust my room, which was a simple, but detailed task. I came out to my house father and asked for my room to be inspected. I had worked hard and was looking forward to passing inspection and being released from my chore. You just could not walk away from a chore like that. You had to be released. My houseparent put a white glove on for the inspection and came to my room. With one swipe on the main dresser, he looked at the white glove and said it was dirty. Do it again. Then he walked away. I was furious because I felt it was clean, so in protest I sat down in a chair and fell asleep for about twenty minutes.

Then I went back out and said, "Sir, will you check me again?"

Again, he came with a white glove and wiped three or four spots and said, "Good work, Maitland."

He released me and walked away. I said nothing about it, but in my heart I said, "You big hypocrite." More bitterness, I guess.

The Letter

One time, I did say my thoughts audibly. That was not a good idea, but I could not hold it in anymore. Here is the scoop! I was not the best letter writer, but I loved to get mail. I still do today. To get mail, you had to write to someone so they would write back. Our mail bag was in our kitchen pantry. We would place the letter in the bag, and they would pick the bag up the next day when the meal truck came to our home. This particular Saturday, I had written two letters and went to the mailbag and put them in like everyone else did. They would be collected from everyone and sent out. The problem was I forgot to put a stamp on one of the letters and noticed it when I put my letters in the bag. I took my letter I had forgotten to put a stamp on back to my room. I walked out of the pantry with a letter in my hand. No problem. Right? Wrong!

That night, we just happened to have a student home meeting, which we did on a monthly basis with our houseparents and everyone in the home. We had a president and vice president of the home. It was like a debriefing in the Army when they would discuss school memos and deal with the running of our home.

All was going well until our housemother said in front of everyone, "What do you think of Maitland going in to the mail bag with one letter and coming out with two?"

I was stunned and taken by surprise. I knew what she meant and to me it could mean only one thing. Without thinking, the words came out.

"Are you calling me a thief?"

That was it. The next words were "Maitland, to the office." I was so mad I cannot even remember my punishment. I guess I ended that meeting. More bitterness.

Sometimes, I would get into trouble and be given extra work and would ask, "What did I do?" The response many times was, "If you do not know, we are not going to tell you." More bitterness.

Scallops

The school wanted us to have a well-balanced diet, which was wonderful, but I ate foods I never heard before: mush, succotash, bulls' eyes, chow chow, and scallops. Two or three times a year during my high school years at Rock Ridge, we would get this food called scallops. At first I was curious, but I had a problem when I ate them.

A few hours later I would start burping eggs, and then I would throw up. I appealed to my houseparent but to no avail. The following times, we were served scallops; the same thing happened again and again. It was the only food that I could not keep down. Maybe it was because they had to be cooked in an institutional way to be sent out to 1,500 boys in the homes. I do not know. I knew we could bounce them off the floor and catch them. I dreaded the scallop day. I begged not to have to eat them, but I had to and would always get sick. They said I was faking it. Finally, after a number of times, they believed me; and I could pass on scallops. I have not eaten one to this day even though my wife enjoys them and begs me to try one. I decline, and I do not get sick. More bitterness.

The Swat

There was a time when I was in my senior home, Rock Ridge, which I will never forget. There was a division of our school called the Home Life Division that dealt with all major behavioral problems in all the approximately one hundred student homes in the school. Of course, being immature kids, we called it the Gestapo. That was unkind, but they were feared by all. The head of the Home Life Division was a serious, stern-looking man whom I respected like my uncle, but I never wanted to end up in his office. One day, at Rock Ridge, Home Life pulled in, and when they got out of the car, they all had suits on. We knew it was serious, but we did not know who was in trouble. I believed it was the "big three." (If you are reading this and went to the school during those years, you will know what I mean.)

Everyone in our home was gathered together in one of the downstairs mud rooms where we changed our clothes after coming in from outside. When the big three, as I remembered it, walked in, they had a large paddle with them. Then they spoke, "Last weekend, when our relief weekend houseparents stayed at Rock Ridge, someone had stolen some articles from the weekend help." They wanted these articles back and now. They had us, one at a time, bend over and put our hands on a bench and gave us a swat. One of the men was a former football player who was feared the most. I got my swat from another man, and it was the hardest swat I ever received in my life. He may have been older, but he knew the art form of giving a swat.

When Home Life was finished, they told us that we had twenty minutes to find out who stole the articles, or we would go through this same process again. They promptly walked out and left us boys alone to discuss the matter. Besides having intensely warm backsides when they walked out, we had no idea who did it. We did know one thing though: we were not going through that process again. This is when I saw the real power of the pecking order and peer pressure. I cannot tell you how, but in twenty minutes, the person who did it had confessed and was turned in. The big three of Home Life got back in their car and left, never to return to Rock Ridge again. Today, I have to admit, it was a stroke of genius in crime solving, but at that time for me it meant more bitterness.

I tell you these stories because, in the end, they helped me. The ideal of Milton Hershey School has always been great. It is the humanity of the people that implement these ideals that are sometimes flawed. People like me who are caught in these situations are also flawed. They taught me one of the greatest lessons in life: life is not always fair. The quicker you realize that the better you will learn to cope with the unfairness of life. I think Rudyard Kipling said it best in the poem "If."

"If"

If you can keep your head when all about you
    Are losing theirs and blaming it on you,
If you can trust yourself when all men doubt you,
    But make allowance for their doubting too;
If you can wait and not be tired by waiting,

Or being lied about, don't deal in lies,
Or being hated, don't give way to hating,
    And yet don't look too good, nor talk too wise:

If you can dream—and not make dreams your master;
    If you can think—and not make thoughts your aim;
If you can meet with Triumph and Disaster
    And treat those two impostors just the same;
If you can bear to hear the truth you've spoken
    Twisted by knaves to make a trap for fools,
Or watch the things you gave your life to, broken,
    And stoop and build 'em up with worn-out tools:

If you can make one heap of all your winnings
    And risk it on one turn of pitch-and-toss,
And lose, and start again at your beginnings
    And never breathe a word about your loss;
If you can force your heart and nerve and sinew
    To serve your turn long after they are gone,
And so hold on when there is nothing in you
    Except the Will which says to them: "Hold on!"

If you can talk with crowds and keep your virtue,
    Or walk with Kings—nor lose the common touch,
If neither foes nor loving friends can hurt you,
    If all men count with you, but none too much;
If you can fill the unforgiving minute
    With sixty seconds' worth of distance run,
Yours is the Earth and everything that's in it,
    And—which is more—you'll be a Man, my son!

        —By Rudyard Kipling
        (Source: www.poetryfoundation.org, 2016)
        [Source: *A Choice of Kipling's Verse*, 1943]

It took me years to deal with my bitterness. When I became a Christian, my perspective changed, and my bitterness gave way to understanding that God allows these things and greater difficulties, such as the death of a loved one, to make us stronger in a world that can be tough to live in. People deal with life's unfairness in many ways. I chose to deal with mine this way, and it helped me turn my stumbling blocks into stepping stones. You can always tell a bitter person when they make excuses, blame others, and play the victim card. This is one of the problems in our American society. Life is rough. Deal with it or it will ruin you, or, better yet, you will use your bitterness to ruin others. Hurt people, hurt people. That is what Autumn Reeder, a teacher friend, taught me. Secondly, it taught me that I wanted to be different. Later when my understanding changed, I began to pursue the ideals that Milton Hershey School stood for in the deed of trust and not the periodic flawed application of its great ideals. Time and perspective have helped me with that. I will never make an unfair world fair. No one can, but I can learn to be a man who is fair in an unfair world and teach others to do the same. Some of the trouble I got into at Rock Ridge I brought on my little-old-flawed self.

The Fight

I was not in many fights; but one day, I was in the basement wrestling with a boy forty pounds heavier than me to increase my wrestling skills. He was a brute of a guy. He did something to make me mad. So without thinking I jumped up and punched him in the face with all of my might. The bad news was he just stood there and looked at me. I never was a fighter nor did I lose my temper often. He proceeded to beat the tar out of me. At least I was smart enough to protect my face like a boxer pinned on the ropes. I bent over so only the top of my head was exposed. He beat on that. I was in a quandary because I felt the lumps coming on the top of my head.

I had to think fast so I pushed away and looked him in the eyes and asked, "Have you had enough?"

He said, "Yes."

We shook hands, and we were friends again. There was no one there to coddle you, and you had to learn to survive by your fists or your wits. That day, I learned to use my wits and pick my battles. Sometimes, you can beat a skunk, but I am telling you that it is just not worth it.

The Friendship

When I was at Hershey, I made many friends. A few were best friends like Jimmy McCauley and Don Gates. But I learned a great lesson about friendships with a guy who became my roommate. His name was Jerry Doyle, and he was the funniest guy I had ever met. We just hit it off so well. I grew up in Butler, Pennsylvania, and he grew up not far away in Pittsburgh. We were good buddies like Jimmy and Don would become in my life.

The problem came when the other guys became jealous of our friendship and started to call us Mutt and Jeff. The pecking order could be cruel at times, and even though we were good friends, we decided to change rooms to stop all the heckling and teasing. It worked in light of the teasing, but we were never really close friends again. I realized later that good friends are a gift from God and are often hard to find in life. The lesson I learned is that I would never let other people interfere with my friendships unless it was for my spiritual welfare. We should not let other people control and monopolize our friendships. We should be able to share our friendships and have the privilege of building friendships that last a life time. Life is short. Cherish your friendships.

My buddies; Jerry Doyle, Steve Castleberry
and myself around 9th grade.

The Great Escape

There were not too many homeboys who did not have any thoughts of running away. I wanted to, but I was too big of a chicken and feared my uncle and what would happen if I made it the 250 miles to home. But once, just once, three of us guys got brave enough to "hook-out," a term used often in the school and frowned upon greatly by the school. With no car, we could not go very far. We figured that we would go up the road about two miles to this secluded place called Arnts Sub Base because it was open late at night. We made a grand plan and picked a night when we felt the houseparents would least suspect it. After bed check, we would sneak out. We synchronized our watches, and when we felt the time was right, we stuffed our beds with blankets and pillows to make it look like we were still there. Original, huh? So we went out through the farthest door from where the houseparents stayed, propped the door open with a little rock, and off we went.

For the next couple of hours, we felt free. We went down across the field, across the creek, and up the dark pathway to Arnts Sub Base. It was a dark night. I am sure we planned it that way. We talked most of the way—first at a whisper then in our normal voices when we were far enough away. We had done it! We finally had "hooked-out." It was quite an experience. We were walking and talking three abreast up this dark field along the road and having a great time.

All of a sudden, two of us looked away; and when we looked back, the guy in the center had disappeared. Vanished! It was scary, like in a movie, and who could we tell because we had "hooked-out" and would be in big trouble. At first, we did not know what to do. How does one of your buddies just disappear on a dark night when all three of you were walking almost shoulder to shoulder? Without knowing it, we had walked over a square, four-foot-deep storm culvert with no grate on it. The two of us on the ends had walked on the edge of it, but the middle guy hit it square on and dropped into the hole, which explains why he disappeared so quickly. He was not hurt. We got him out and had a good time the rest of the way but walked more carefully, mind you.

We got to Arnts Sub Base, ordered our food, acted like the locals, and had a great time eating our subs. We had eaten institutional food for so long that a sub was the best thing ever. We made our way to our student home and our re-entry back into the world of Milton Hershey, hoping the smell of onions and Italian dressing would not give us away. When we got back to our escape door, we could tell it was tampered with. We got to our rooms, and all of our beds had been turned back. We knew we had been caught. In true Rock Ridge fashion, we had to suffer the night waiting for our consequences. There were always consequences. I do not remember how we got punished, but I began to pick up on a pattern in my life experience so far: I almost always got caught. At the time, I thought it was a real bummer, but it has always kept me from going too far from the sidewalk and straying far from the path.

People who get caught are blessed people in the end if they learn from it. At first, I thought it was just that destiny thing,; but later on, I realized it was God keeping me on a short rope. It is when you do not get caught often that you should worry because you will think that you can get away with anything. I was a "get caughter." I am glad that I was, and I hope I always will be. It means God cares about me. "For whom the Lord loveth he chasteneth" (Heb. 12:6a). Do not let anyone tell you that "hooking-out" was not fun. Sin is fun, but the price tag of "hooking-out" was too high for me so I never did it again.

The Lump

Bullying was common in the orphanage, but it was dealt with strongly if caught. Like I said, it is not the ideals that are flawed but the flawed nature of human beings that causes the problem.

In ninth grade, I was pretty small, five foot two and eighty-five pounds. If you are a minnow in a shark tank, you better learn how to survive. Squealing (telling the houseparent) was not a survival technique because the ideals of the system will not protect you when no one is around.

One day, we were playing football on a grassy field by a pond about 200 yards from the house. The boys whom I was playing with were all much bigger than I was. We had a great time until we finished the game and the big guys got bored. Someone said, "Let's throw someone in the pond!" Guess who got that honor? Me. I was smallest guy in the group, and there was no fighting it. I was outnumbered and before I knew it, I was going head first into the pond. There was no harm done except that they threw me in at the end of the pond, and when I went into the water, I hit my head on the cement abutment about a foot below. When I came up, they could tell something was wrong because I was pretty dazed. Then everyone was scared and asked if I was okay or, more importantly, whether I would squeal and get them all in trouble. Within an hour, I had a large hematoma lump on my eyebrow/forehead area about the size of a baseball. When I was asked what happened, I said I fell into the pond and hit my head. I did not squeal; instead, I chose to keep my mouth shut. That is the way it was in the orphanage.

A few months later, we were playing football again, and the bullying came up again. Being small I was the one selected. This time, one of the top dogs in the group put his arm around me and said, "Don't touch Maitland. He's okay." No one touched me after that. I was not a squealer, but I developed a great distaste for bullying. When I was older and one of the big dogs, I did not do it myself or participate in any group efforts. I just did not have the stomach for it.

One of the few times I did not get caught was a Saturday when the weekend relief help was on duty; and in many cases, they were more relaxed than the regular houseparents. I decided to raid the pantry for everyone on Saturday afternoon. I was able to sneak into the kitchen pantry and take a stash of cookies. In those days, we had what we called "a cow"—a large refrigerated unit, which housed large bags of white and chocolate milk. It had weighted levers so when you lift the arm, the milk would come out by gravity feed. All the homes had them, and they would only be used by permission and at meal times. I grabbed two of the silver pitchers and filled them. I sneaked away with the goods to share with the other guys. It sounds silly, but stuff like this made the boring day in the orphanage somewhat exciting. It was called "raiding the pantry." The problem was I could not find anyone. After a search, I ran down the seldom-used back stairwell to the basement where I found the gang. I hollered, "I raided the pantry!" and came to share the spoils. They all said, "Shhh!" I wondered what they were up to. They were waiting for someone in the game room to do something, and when one of the guys gave the signal, they ran in and beat the tar out of the guy they did not like. It was cruel to watch, and I could not take part in it.

I was learning how cruel kids could be in life. Life can be cruel. Watch your back. A normal day in the unit or at school could turn into conflict or a fight at any moment. This is one of the ways I learned about the pecking order. Sports, the classroom, and the playground were the other areas. In every grouping of people, there is a big dog that everyone yielded to. If there is no clear-cut big dog at first, there will be a shuffle until it is decided. As the little pond joins the bigger pond, a big dog will rise up. You learned to know where your place and role were. Put simply, you learned when to stand, when to back down, and when to fight. Teasing and making fun of each other was common place in the home. You had to learn how to take it, when to give it back, and when to be quiet.

My problem was that I was painfully shy except around my closest friends. It was hard for me to exert leadership because I did not know I had it in me until years later. What I did learn is how to function in and use the pecking order to my advantage and to survive. Periodically, I would take a stand if I felt backed into a corner and had no way out, but most of the time I used the art of negotiation and blending in to survive in an all-boys school.

Here is a final story that happened to me when I was home on vacation during my sophomore year. It may seem silly, but it proves my point. Probably starting around the age of three, I always liked girls. My uncle's brother, Zeke, had a horse barn. On vacation, I loved to go to the horse barn. Girls liked horses so I liked horses. We would sit in the tack room joking and having a fun time cleaning all the stalls and feeding the horses. I had just gotten to know my neighbor, Buzzy. He was loud and bombastic, and he wore combat boots. I loved him and got a kick out of him. He was a personality—ethnic to the core. Slovak, I believe. His girlfriend came up from Pittsburgh, and she was a beauty. She came to the barn every day because she liked horses. For some reason, Buzzy did not like horses. We were all having great fun, and then it happened. One day, Buzzy's girlfriend and I looked at each other, and we knew it; we liked each other. It was not something we said… we just understood. Maybe it came from understanding the pecking order. We knew we had a problem, and there was nothing to do to stop it. You cannot plan a crush; it just happens.

I thought about it and marched up to Buzzy's house, which happened to be across the street, and told him I had fallen for his girlfriend and she had fallen for me. I did not know how it happened—it just happened. Buzzy blew his top and verbally tore into me. We became enemies in an instant. He "called me out." I knew what that meant from the orphanage. He told me to meet him behind the barn the next day at noon, and we would fight it out. I left his house not wanting to fight Buzzy because he was my friend, he was big, and he threatened to kick the snot out of me with his big Army boots. Well, noon came the next day and—call me crazy—I showed up behind the barn. Buzzy was there in his Army boots, and he looked threatening. He brought another kid with him named Tommy. I never met Tommy before, but he had long hair and looked scary. Buzzy said he was going to let Tommy beat me up and do his light work. I was so scared. I negotiated my way out of the fight somehow, and we ended up playing baseball together that day. I regained my friendship with Buzzy, and Tommy became one of my best friends.

Learn and understand the pecking order in life, who to fear and who not to fear, who to honor and who not to honor (do not honor bullies), and who to follow and who not to follow. I learned to fear the Lord. All this pecking order stuff fell into perspective. Romans 8:31b says, "If God be for us, who can be against us?" When you realize that God is the ruler of the biggest pond in the entire universe, all the other ponds flow into His pond. So if I walk with him, I am safe. Proverbs 29:25b says, "The fear of man bringeth a snare." I am telling you all of this because I know what that fear felt like in the earlier years. I learned that fear does not have to control me. When God controls me, then there is no pecking order that can control me. I learned that God loves me. I John 4:18a says, "There is no fear in love but perfect love casteth out fear." While life is still cruel, this truth will help you live in a cruel world but not to become cruel yourself.

Old Senior Hall

When you come to Hershey Park, if you look to the north, you will see a large "Welcome to Hershey" laid out in white stone on the hillside. It was there in 1960 when I came, and it is still there today. Behind it, at the top, is the school on the hill. Everyone who graduated from Milton Hershey for the first seventy years spent their high school years at what was then known as Senior Hall. Senior Hall became an iconic figure through the years. When the school shifted its main campus to the other side of town, Old Senior Hall fell into disrepair and was in danger of becoming just a memory. When John O'Brien became president at MHS, he convinced the school to give Senior Hall an eighty-five-million-dollar renovation. Shops in the original design included carpentry, electronics, plumbing, auto mechanic, and printing. The face of the front was restored to its original brick, and the main parts of the building were saved and refurbished. New classrooms, an Olympic size swimming pool, and a beautiful new dining hall were added. Senior Hall is now an intermediate school capable of housing eight hundred students. They did an amazing job in bringing Old Senior Hall back to life.

I tell you all this because I was able to get a look during the renovations when I walked into the original lobby, the auditorium, and gym. My memories and my emotions went crazy even though I had not been in Senior Hall for thirty years. I could not fight back the tears and the flashbacks of so many great and yet, at times, difficult memories. I could take you to the history class I was in when John F. Kennedy was shot. Besides the home, I spent most of my time from sixth through twelfth grades at Senior Hall.

School and Home Life

These are my memories from life in the Senior Homelife Division at Milton Hershey School. We got up early, did our chores, had breakfast, and got ready for school. We had six sets of clothing: pajamas, barn clothes, play clothes, house clothes, school clothes, and church clothes. You were always checked for proper attire whenever you left the home for school, church, or town privileges. We went to the fitting center twice each year. Milton Hershey had its own clothing center. I loved it and always looked forward to going. Once, when I was at the Main (the fourth and fifth grade home), I was getting new shoes, and I wanted slip-on shoes. My feet were too small, and they only had tie shoes in my size. When I went back to my home, I prayed that God would let my feet grow so I could get slip-on shoes. As I grew, I moved into slip-on shoes, and today I wear a size thirteen. I did not realize it at the time, but the school only bought the best. I was an orphan boy going around in Botany five hundred suits and clothes. Picture 1,500 boys going to church in Botany 500 suits, white shirts, and ties. It was impressive when we were all together. We had to wear Florsheim wing tip shoes, and I hated them. It was like someone took a drill and drilled a hundred holes in the top of the shoes with a 1/8" drill bit. Today I wear them all the time.

Every clothing category had a standard and a certain look. As they wore out, they would move from church clothes to school clothes, to houses clothes, to play clothes, to barn clothes, and then they would go out the door. If we were short in any of these areas, we were issued new clothes. I really enjoyed picking out my clothes, especially the suits. School attire was a dress collared shirt, dress slacks, and dress shoes. All of this was paid for by the generosity of Milton Snavely Hershey.

To go to school every day, Milton Hershey furnished each home with the most unusual vehicles I had ever seen. They ordered a station wagon that could seat fifteen people. It was like a stretch limo before they became popular, and they came in all different colors. People from out of town would always stare when we went by. When we all pulled in at the football game, it looked like a party for millionaires. I guess we were *rich*, but we did not see it that way at the time.

We were at school by eight in the morning, and spent the rest of the day at Senior Hall until 2:30 p.m. with a hot lunch for everyone. It was during this time that MHS gave us the best education and the best teachers that money could buy. I wish I could say I gave it my best, but I did not wake up and realize what I had until my junior year. I was a B student, but I could have done better except I had my eye on sports. Probably my most challenging area was reading. I was not a great reader like my wife, Bonnie, whom I married years later. Now I know those who read, lead. I had to do some catching up later in life. I loved math, history, and science. I still remember the colors of the rainbow by "Roy G Biv."

I did not realize at the time that Senior Hall, the school on the hill, was like a polishing wheel and I was the rough diamond. They taught us everything. At mealtime, we had to do everything according to what etiquette expert Amy Vanderbilt said. Our choir teacher gave us the class on etiquette in small groups. He was meticulous about everything including: how a table was set, how to pull out a chair for a lady, passing the food (always to the right), placing a napkin on your lap, not putting your elbows on the table, chewing with your mouth closed, taking what you will eat and eating what you take, how to hold your silverware, never burping (try to get a bunch of boys to do that), always cleaning up afterwards, pushing your chair in, and wiping your mouth. This paid off later in life when I needed it.

Senior Hall also had its own doctors' and dentists' offices. The dentists were so good. I still have many of my fillings today. I dreaded going to the dentist because he always found a cavity to fill. I remember those shots of Novocain and the pretty nurse who held my hand because those needles seemed to be a foot long. I have always been a wimp with needles; however, in the orphanage, you could not let anyone know.

We even had our own barber shop at Senior Hall, which seemed to be up in one of the towers you see when you look up at Senior Hall from the park. Once a month, we would go up the tower to Zook the barber. Every month, we would ask to get it cut a certain way, and every month it was the same cut. You could always spot a homeboy by his haircut. We used to laugh and say it was just like getting a bowl put on your head and having your hair cut accordingly. It always had to be off the ears and off the collar. Zook was a great guy, and it was always fun to see him. I am sure Zook was under orders as to how to cut our hair. Things like this helped to break the monotony of everyday life.

Lunch

When you feed hundreds of boys at once, it is organized chaos—with an emphasis on the organized. Everything had a system. Every table had a teacher or staff as head, and we would sit twenty to a long table. The boy on the right went up to get the family-style food and seconds if there were any, which there usually were. The boy on the left was the cleanup man, and at the end of the meal we passed our plates and silverware up to him. We wiped the table and waited for dismissal.

One time, at lunch, I was sitting about half-way down the table with a stack of bread in front of me. One of the guys said, "Maitland, pass some bread." We were never allowed to throw food at the table. I guess it was a good rule because if you let eight hundred boys at Senior Hall throw food, it could easily turn into the food fights you see in the movies. The head of our table that day was our math teacher. He was an extremely stocky man who ate with his head down most of the time. I heard the call for bread from the boy on his left. I decided it was too far to pass so I flung the bread like a Frisbee, but it got away from me and was on target to hit our math teacher smack in the middle of his head. When I saw it flying up the table, I instantly got this sick feeling because if it hit our teacher, I would be in big trouble. Just before it hit him in the head my buddy snatched it out of the air. The teacher had his head down eating and never knew a thing. I am glad my buddy had good eye-hand coordination. The rest of the time lunch was pretty boring.

All this happened at Senior Hall, but the main part of life was our studies. Some of my teachers I do not remember, some I feared, some I respected, and some touched my life deeply. They all helped me along my journey to a good education. For most of my high school years, I blended in and went with the flow. I did not get into any trouble and got along pretty well with my classmates. I pretty much stayed invisible. I was small for my age and could have started a year later because I graduated at age seventeen. I was extremely shy and struggled with confidence. I was also terrified to stand before a crowd or to be singled out.

One day, I was not paying attention during our homeroom opening exercises when we were reciting "The Pledge of Allegiance."

The teacher said, "Maitland, since you are not paying attention, you lead us in 'The Pledge of Allegiance'."

The room grew silent, and all eyes turned to me. I knew the pledge by heart, but I froze and nothing came out. I could not remember a word.

My buddy leaned over and whispered the first line, "I pledge allegiance."

I responded, "I pledge allegiance."

Nothing.

Then my buddy said, "To the flag."

I said, "To the flag."

Nothing.

The teacher in disgust said, "Maitland, sit down."

I was crushed. My Achilles heel was that I froze in public. I also purposed at that time that when I was in charge, I would never embarrass someone publicly unless that person forced me to. I know I've missed many opportunities because of this extreme shyness.

Other times, at school, I was just plain scared, especially of Mr. Balicic. Even his name was scary to me. Mr. Balicic was a great history teacher. Everyone was afraid of him except for Ben Riggin who was the toughest kid in our class. He was the guy who wanted to beat me up in fifth grade. He was tough and had a reputation. Ben decided to fall asleep in Mr. Balicic's class. When Mr. Balicic taught, all eyes were on him. While he was teaching, he walked to the back of the room, so we turned in our chairs not to lose eye contact with him. He went to the sink in the back, grabbed a sponge, soaked it with water, and slowly walked up the aisle all the time he was teaching. When he came to Ben Riggin's desk, he squeezed the sponge on his head and flipped the desk over with Ben in it. You could have heard a pin drop. Mr. Balicic continued teaching, but

Ben never fell asleep in class again. By the way, I got good grades in history; but one time, I got in trouble. Mr. Balicic stepped out of the class, and I dropped my pencil which then rolled out into the middle of the aisle. As I leaned over to pick it up, Mr. Balicic walked in and thought I was cheating. There was no explaining with Mr. Balicic. I was called to the front of the room and had to put my hands on the desk. I was told to watch the birdie, a stuffed bird we had hanging above the chalkboard. Then he proceeded to give me two hard swats with the paddle, and I was told to sit down. I guess I can say I was now an elite member of Mr. Balicic's Birdie Club. I know there were many members throughout the years.

Mr. Storm was a new teacher when I started high school who taught economics. We always tried to get him off track at the beginning of class by asking him what he had eaten for breakfast. He was a tough teacher and smarter than all of us. I admired him greatly and learned much from him. Secretly, we all called him Stormy.

In ninth grade, I went into the college prep program and took classes to prepare for college as well as entering a shop trade. The school had all kinds of trade shops. Senior Hall had its own full-fledged vo-tech school as well as a regular education school. I wanted to take carpentry so bad, but I was not assigned there. The counselors enrolled me in a shop I did not want because of quotas. It was one of those times I felt backed up against the wall, and I had to overcome my shyness and speak my mind. It worked. I did not get carpentry, but I ended up in automotive shop and was satisfied. Actually, it turned out great. Years later, when I became a preacher, I had a practical, mechanical side and could work with my hands—something that preachers are not always known for. The trades provide us a practical side of life—to be handy with tools and become more of a problem solver when things break in life and need to be fixed.

I enjoyed shop a lot. We would have two weeks of class and then two weeks of shop. Mr. Buck and Mr. Daubert were great—especially Mr. Daubert. I am sure he would be proud of me today if he were alive. He was a gentle soul and a great mentor in the shop.

He was one of the men I admired a lot. School was great, and when I graduated, I had the opportunity to go to college or into the trades. I chose the trades and went to an automotive/auto-body, tech-school college called Vale Tech. God had other plans, and He used Milton Hershey to prepare me academically and practically for my life calling. You have no idea how often I refer back to what I learned at Milton Hershey.

12 years old on Confirmation Day at the Lutheran Church.

Church

I was born Catholic and went to St. Paul Parochial School, but when my parents died, that all changed. My Aunt and Uncle Stirling were Lutheran, and since they were the ones who took me in under their roof during vacation, I became Lutheran.

Everyone at Milton Hershey was required to attend a nondenominational service with all 1,500 of us (plus staff) at 9 a.m. every Sunday. Following the MHS service, we could go to the church of our choice as that was Mr. Hershey's wish. I wanted to seek religious knowledge, but I guess I just did not get it. My shyness played a large role here also. I tried out to be a Scripture reader in the main service, but when I stood up in tryouts and tried to read, no words came out, just air.

The man in charge said, "Maitland, try again."

I tried again but no words, just air.

The man said, "Sit down, Maitland."

That was the end of that.

Milton Hershey is not a Christian school, but there were Christians working there. Milton Hershey wanted his students to seek God in their own way. Pastor Kevin Brown, one of the first Afro-American students at the school was led to the Lord by Mr. Huggendubbler, the head of the print shop. My time for accepting Christ would come later after I graduated.

Can you imagine that forty years later this shy boy would stand before 2,500 students and guests on the MHS one hundred-year anniversary homecoming and have the privilege of sharing the love of God and the gospel to all who would listen? It was one of the high points in my life to come back to the school I loved and share my faith and the great opportunity that Hershey had given to us as students and alumni by preaching on a poem I learned during my senior year, "A Bag of Tools." This was not bad for a boy who, when he had once opened his mouth, nothing came out but air. I give God the glory.

CHAPTER 7

When You're Number 41

God used another area of the school to begin the process of my overcoming shyness and fear of people, and that area for me was sports. This part of the book may be longer, so I hope that you will enjoy it, even if you do not like sports. Sports, especially wrestling, put the maraschino cherry on my character so that later in life I could overcome my shyness in order to find my life calling.

Neither of my brothers was athletic nor did they have any interest in sports. I took a liking to sports right away, and everything in this area I learned in the sand lot from eight-years-old and after. When I went to ninth grade, I had the opportunity to try out for high school sports. I strongly wanted to play basketball and football, but at five foot two and eighty-five pounds, it did not look good. I was too small for basketball and too light for football. I even put weight in my back pockets, but they caught me and told me I was too small to play football. I said I had good hands and could catch a football, but they still said no, which was heartbreaking to me. I did not know that shortly after high school, I would grow to six foot two and 230 pounds. I remember that John Kolb, from the Steelers, asked me one time if I had played professional football. I just chuckled. I needed that when I was in ninth grade. I guess I was a late bloomer.

I tried everything from baseball to drill team and trombone lessons. I finally talked the music teacher into giving me trombone lessons, but I forgot to go to my first lesson a week later. I was so embarrassed that I had forgotten my lesson that I never went back; the world may have lost a great trombone player. I guess you could call it a sport if I made the band and played at football games.

I was destined to live my life in the shadows. When you are in a school like Milton Hershey, you want to leave a mark in some way or to be noticed for some accomplishment. I figured out later in my life that most of the world feels that way—lost in obscurity.

Theodore Roosevelt said most people live in the twilight between victory and defeat. I just did not know how to get there— to Victory, that is. I never considered myself a coward, but I was just terribly afraid to step out of the shadows for fear of failure. There is a difference between the two. There was one time I considered myself a coward when I was in the hallway between classes. At Senior Hall, one of the cool kids was going down the stairs, turned, and said something mean about my mother. In my mind I wanted to run down the stairs and punch him, but I did not. I was a coward, and it still bothers me some today. Yes, I know I probably would have been in big trouble. There were a few things I loved and honored in my life at that time, and my mother was one of them, so I felt I had disgraced my mother's name. I see him when I go to homecoming, but I have no anger toward him today. I just wish that I would have had the courage to confront him that day and have him take back what he said. Even if this would help me begin to face my fears and eventually try to overcome them, I hope I never lose courage like that again in my life but rather face and handle my problems in a godly manner.

How does an eighty-five-pound weakling make his mark in a school so large? He chooses the toughest and the most prestigious sport in school: wrestling. This was only because it was the only sport left, and I did not have the voice to make the Glee Club choir. They also did not have cuts for wrestling in ninth grade though I had a little problem on the first day of practice. They had roll call and called out all forty boys' names that had come out for the sport.

When the coach finished, I went over and said, "Sir, you forgot to call my name, Maitland."

The coach said, "Oh!"

He looked down the list and did not find my name. He said, "Okay," and wrote my name down in the forty-first spot. That is how my illustrious career in wrestling began, starting at number forty-one on the ninth grade roster. They did not care whether I stayed or left. I did not see myself as a coward (except for that one time in the hallway), but I was in danger of being vanilla, blending in and being forgotten before I could leave my mark in some way. I wonder how many people feel the way I felt that day. I wanted to have purpose and meaning and have people respect me for something I did. By the way, vanilla is my favorite ingredient, but I did not want my life to be vanilla.

Wrestling was my best and only shot at distinction so I committed myself to it fully. By the end, you may think I committed myself too much, but please show grace to a foolish, determined, but painfully shy boy desperate to come out of his shell and be heard. I started, as I said, at the bottom of the list. Actually I started below the bottom (number forty-one) since my name was not on the list. One mantra that would keep me going—the words of Don Witman in the sixth grade wrestling tournament when he put his arm around me and said, "Dave, some day you are going to be a great wrestler." That one sentence of praise filled me with hope and drive. I was in his office, and he said, "Dave, one day you will help to win the Lehigh Trophy."

Mr. Witman was a phenomenal coach, and the Lehigh Trophy was the greatest honor for our private school. This trophy was equal to state because we could not wrestle in state because we were a private school. Central Pennsylvania was the powerhouse in wrestling, and they went to the Lehigh Tournament. Wrestling was the biggest sport at the time, and for our school to win the Lehigh Tournament would be the crème brûlée of our school. If our school won, they would bring the wrestlers up on stage and present the Lehigh Trophy at the Senior Hall assembly in that famous auditorium. Now, how does a bug on the wall earn the right to step on that stage in such honor? Work! Work! Work!

I had three goals that were under my mantra. The first goal was to make the varsity wrestling team and wear the brown and gold. The second goal was to win my varsity letter, which was harder yet. I would have to beat six opponents. I would receive two points each win for a total of twelve points to earn my varsity letter. I would earn three points if I pinned someone, but that was not going to happen. Twelve points in one season was my goal. My third goal was that before I graduated, I wanted to be a part of winning the Lehigh Trophy—even if it was one point and to stand on that stage as a wrestler.

As far as being a great wrestler, well, that just felt good. A number of my teammates were great wrestlers like the Rupp brothers, John Beekman, and in years past, Bobby Fehrs. I would be satisfied if my five foot two eighty-five-pound piece of vanilla could reach these three lofty goals.

This goes to show you the power of encouragement and what it can do in someone's life. Coaches today motivate by berating and even cursing at their players. Yes, discipline is necessary, but I feel we fall too short on encouragement. I do not think that Mr. Witman was lying when he said I could be a great wrestler. I believe he saw something in me behind my shyness and my being a face in the crowd (vanilla). He wanted to bring it out, and he felt wrestling was the way to do it.

There is no tougher sport than wrestling! When you are on that mat, all eyes are on you and your opponent. Everyone is depending on you. You cannot hide, and your every move on that mat is under a microscope. You had to be in the best shape and even then there was so much physical exertion given on the mat during certain matches. It was hard to walk off the mat even in victory.

I worked all year round and paced myself, learning everything about wrestling that I could. I even practiced in my bedroom before lights out, perfecting my sit out and switch move over and over. In the off-season, I had a workout schedule: running one day and lifting weights the next, not for bulk but for muscle tone and endurance. At first it was rough, and I remember when I finally made it to the varsity wrestling room. We wrestled round robins, three circles, 95, 103, and 172. We matched up then rotated to all three circles, one minute rotate, on and on it went. I took a beating. One practice I leaned against the wall on the floor whimpering so no one would see me because I was too exhausted to walk out. I remember the conditioning, the suicides in the gym, and running up and down the stairs in the balcony of the gym. This took place through ninth and tenth grades. While I was getting better, I had one problem: I had to deal with my shyness and confidence. The JV players and the scrubs (that was me) went to our first scrimmage. At this point, Mr. Witman was no longer the head coach because he had been promoted to become one of the principals in one of the divisions of our school. Mr. Faidley had become the coach. Another man, who was the JV coach, took us to our first scrimmage. He would report to Coach Faidley on our progress.

When it came to my turn to wrestle, I froze. It was not my opponent. It was the crowd… I could not handle the crowd. It was like stage fright. I had headgear on, and the crowd's screaming echoed in my ear… and I just froze. I lost, and in the locker room that coach called me a yellow-bellied chicken and a scared rabbit. He basically turned his back on me and made me feel worthless. Have you ever had anyone give up on you like that? I knew then not everyone in my life was going to be a Don Witman so I better deal with it. I licked my wounds that day, but I did not have a plan to fix it.

The summer of my tenth grade year, two things happened. One day at Rock Ridge, the phone rang and one of the wrestlers in a cottage about three hundred yards away wanted to know if I would come over every Saturday and practice with him. His name was Byron Ramsey. He was almost as good as the Rupp brothers and the cockiest kid on the wrestling team. He wanted to practice with me because I was ninety-five pounds, and he was about 103-112. I got permission to go, but what was I thinking?

Every week, Byron threw me around like a rag doll, and his trash talking was endless. Every week I went again, and every week he worked me over. One time, in a takedown, I heard my knee go crack, crack, and crack. It swelled up like a softball, and I had to sit out for a couple of weeks. Then I went back again. I must have been crazy, but I did not want to be a coward so I went. Week after week, it went on, and then things began to change. We became buddies, and I started to check his moves. He was developing me into a defensive wrestler, and his cockiness did not bother me anymore. It was not my style, but dealing with intimidation is part of wrestling. Byron helped me with that, and I learned how to deal with him and his cockiness, which would come in handy in the future.

I still had the problem of dealing with the crowd. But when the referee would say wrestle, I learned to fire across the mat and use a single-leg takedown that I had worked on endlessly for speed and accuracy. When I took my opponent down and made the first strike, the shyness would leave me, I would be okay for the rest of the match, and the crowd would not bother me. It was weird, but it worked.

Wrestle-offs came, and I began to win. When we did round robins in practice, I held my own. In fact, I became second in my weight class on varsity behind my good friend Jimmy McCauley. He was better than me, but I could now hold my own thanks to the summer with Byron Ramsey.

I made the varsity team my junior year and was second on the depth chart at ninety-five pounds and was now five foot seven, which was tall for my age. Since I was growing, it was harder to stay in my weight class. My natural weight would have been 130 pounds. I started watching my weight in June at the end of my sophomore year. I cut out potatoes and bread from my diet and was around 98-100 pounds at the start of the season.

The Match

After school, I went down to the locker room, and my best friend Jimmy McCauley was starting the first match at ninety-eight pounds. There was a problem, though; Jimmy was shorter than me and solid muscle. He was ten pounds overweight, and there was no way he was going to make the weigh-in by six in the evening. We were in a jam because we would have to forfeit our match, so they approached me. I am sure they were desperate, and I said, "Don't worry. I will make weight by weigh in." So I put on a rubber sweat suit and started running around our indoor pool because it was the closest thing to a sauna. I was trying to drop five pounds in two and a half hours. It was tougher than I thought because I was pretty lean before I started. I had to drop it so fast, but I was not going to miss this opportunity. I would check it about every half hour, and my weight was slowly coming down. Then one of the wrestlers told me if I took some Ex-Lax it would help me lose some more. It was chocolate and tasted good. If one piece would work, then the whole box would be better. The coaches never knew about the Ex-Lax. I made weight, barely. The team had their ninety-eight pounder and did not have to forfeit. I had reached my first lofty goal of starting varsity wrestling for the Milton Hershey Spartans.

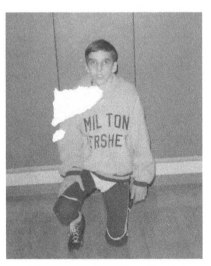

Accomplishing my first goal, starting
varsity my junior year at 95 lbs.

Donning that varsity uniform and that furry gold hoodie pulled over my head was a feeling I cannot explain to you. While it may be for only one match, I was going to lead the team, this glorious incredibly tough team, up the stairs and burst into the gym for the first match of the 1968 season. As I told you, wrestling was big in the central part of the state so I believe the gym was full. When I burst through that door, I felt like I was in the movie "Rudy." The roar was deafening. As we ran out and around the gym, we circled the mat, and our team captain led us in warm up. My heart was coming out of my chest. I felt a feeling of pride and belonging I had never experienced before. As I write this years later, I swell up in tears. The fly on the wall, Mr. Vanilla, number forty-one on the list, two years later had reached his first secret goal and was going to step into the limelight.

The match was a blur. I used my new plan as soon as the referee said, "Wrestle." I shot for a take down, but he shot at the same time, causing us to butt heads which almost knocked me out. After that, everything went downhill quickly. He would take me down, let me up, and take me down again, and instantly tried to pin me. When you are on your back, you learn to bridge on your neck. That is a life skill I learned from wrestling Byron Ramsey, the cockiest kid on our team who also could back it up. At one time, my opponent pounced on my chest to make me collapse to my shoulders and pin me, but I was not going down. I looked at the light most of the match. I was weak from pulling weight so fast. I ended up losing around 14-2, but I was not pinned and gave up three team points rather than six points to a pin. I found out later that my opponent had been a state champ.

My debut was a loss, and the coach paid no attention to me. I cannot tell you how I felt afterwards. I am sure I felt I had failed at my opportunity. Everyone loves a winner. I know one thing, I was not a coward, and when my opponent broke my sword, I beat him with the handle. I had given my best even though I fell short in the world's eyes. I did not make any excuses, and I was not quitting. What lay ahead I did not know.

The next match came, and Jimmy could not make weight again so I wrestled. Before a wrestler goes out on the mat, the team huddles around you to give you encouragement, and since ninety-eight lbs. is the smallest weight class, I was always the first. It really was not encouragement. They would slap you silly to fire you up. One time, the funniest kid on our team got slapped up so much that he ran out so fired up that he tripped on the mat and ran right past the referee and his opponent. He crashed into the opposing team's chairs on the other side of the mat. We laughed so hard. He was such a good wrestler. He was the only guy I knew who could make his opponent give up because of his powerful cross body rides and scissor holds.

When I shot out of that huddle for my second match, I was fired up. When the referee said, "Wrestle." I shot for the take down and got it. Then all the fear left me, and I had no problem the rest of the match. I won the match and was 1-1, three points for our team and two points toward my letter which was my second goal. While that goal still seemed a long way off, I was thankful that the crowd did not bother me, although my coach did not notice me. I was just so happy that I won. I had never won anything in my life, and it felt good.

My best friend just could not make weight, but I was right on the weight every time after that first match. I promise, no Ex-Lax. I wrestled my second match and won. Now I was 2-1. After my third match, I was 3-1. I went out there the same way as I had for the others, shooting for the take down right away. I guess I caught them by surprise, and I learned that surprise can be a great advantage in life.

By now, I was the regular starter and was half way to my second goal. Our match this time was away, and word got around that their ninety-eight-pounder was another state champ. I was scared, I will admit, but you have to do what you have to do. Our lower weights on the team were tough. My other teammates in the lower weight classes were state champ material, and I was a nobody. As my friend and I joked, some people are Hellmann's Mayonnaise (well-known) and some are Smith mayonnaise (unknown). I was the Smith mayonnaise.

When we got to the opponent's gym and weighed in, we found out that there was a line-up change for the other school. Since I was an unknown, they moved their state champ up to 103 and placed another wrestler in the 98-pound class to wrestle me. This way they felt they would sweep the two lower weights. It seemed like a smart plan because one of the Rupp brothers was 103, and he was Hellmann's mayonnaise like their state champ.

After weigh-ins, I did something I had never done before nor ever did again. I ate a lot of junk food for energy. You see, after you weigh-in, it does not matter how much you weigh because you're wrestling within the hour. I ate too much and paid for it terribly. All during the match my opponent kept using the tight waist move on me. By the third period, I thought I was going to heave up all those candy bars I ate. In the end, I won 4-3, and our 103-pounder beat their state champ. We swept the low weights. I went to a 4-1 record and never ate much after weigh-in again. It was after this win that the head coach, Mr. Faidley, began to notice me and compliment me on helping the team. They moved my best friend, Jimmy, to a different weight class, and I became the first-string 98-pounder for the team.

I kept with my plan to go for the single-leg takedown as soon as the match started and won my next two matches. I went to 6-1 and earned my twelve points to win my varsity letter. I had reached the second lofty goal I had secretly set for myself. I cannot tell you what an honor it was to receive that letter at the end of the year; I still have it today. To me, at the time, it was my most cherished possession.

The school provided those wonderful ideal opportunities to build character, friendships, and a sense of honor. In the wrestling room, in the locker room, in Rock Ridge, and in the pecking order is where the ideal meets the real.

In a school like ours, nicknames were very common— sometimes they were to honor and sometimes they were hurtful. When I started out pulling weight at the beginning, I looked pretty bad and the nicknames they gave me were not very complementary.

When I started winning and became the little buddy on the team, they started to call me Spiderman, the popular comic book hero. I liked it, and it felt good to be recognized. Because of the orphanage, I became partial to nicknames and use them often even today with the people to whom I minister. I learned the power of a nickname for good to encourage and for bad to destroy.

When you see a good quality or some character a person exemplifies that is honorable, a good nickname can help him to aspire to it or honor him in the pecking order of life. I never use negative or cruel nicknames to hurt someone or make myself look better. I always try to be honest and not falsely flatter, but inspire because the human nature seems to rise to that. I learned the power of this tool in the orphanage. In fact, I experienced it.

While this was going on, I became real close friends with Don Gates who wrestled at 165 pounds. He was the big guy, and I was the little guy. We were both in the Rock Ridge student home. Don was a no-nonsense, practical guy who had a terrible time at Rock Ridge. We became best of buddies. He looked after me on the wrestling team. Actually years later he said he could always see me as a preacher. He now lives in California and is a doctor. I miss seeing him after all these years.

Another reality at the time was that Milton Hershey School was an all-white school, and Afro-American students would not come to the school for several years. I believe it was my eighth match, and when I went to weigh-in, I realized that my opponent was the first black athlete I had ever wrestled. He was tall and slender like me. I was scared, and my teammates teased me and told me I was going to get beaten. It was new to me, and I was not prejudiced... just scared. When the referee said, "Wrestle," I did what I always did. I shot for the take down, but as he was trying to counter, he poked me in the eye. I was stunned. I chased after him, got the take down, and realized he was just as scared as I was. Sometimes, we are scared of people who seem different from us, and maybe they are scared of us because we are different from them. Maybe that is why we have so much hate and war in this world. I won that day, but my fear had turned into respect—win or lose. I was beginning to gain confidence in myself as well as respect for others. In light of the sports world, my goals would seem tiny. In every one of us, there is a drive to be successful even in small things. I was 41st on the ninth grade depth chart in wrestling. I had met two of my goals, starting on the varsity team and earning my varsity letter with a record of 7-1. I was not cocky; instead, I felt humbled and honored... and then it happened.

I was preparing for my next match, and we were in the practice room going through moves like the fireman's carry when I butted heads with another wrestler in practice. It felt like I hit a brick wall. My head swelled, and I had to go see a doctor. It knocked me out of the lineup for some time. The doctor did not like that I was dropping so much weight. He stepped in and would not let me wrestle in the ninety-five-pound class the rest of the year. That summer, I continued to train. One day, I got a call from Mr. Witman, asking if I would help teach elementary kids some wrestling skills in a clinic he was having. I went and loved it so much. I worked so hard in preparing. It seemed to come natural to teach younger kids. This is when I realized that I had a real love for children and loved teaching and encouraging them.

My senior season rolled around, and the doctor refused to let me wrestle in the 95-pound class. Our team was so strong my senior year. Lower weights were so strong, and I was not able to bump up a weight. I learned a new role—teaching and working out with the 95-pounders my senior year. Periodically I would go to the doctor and plead with him, but he would say no. I loved our school, I loved our team, and reaching two out of my three goals was not so bad. I guess God was teaching me a new lesson: it is not always about me. It is about helping others be the best they can be. You see I prayed to God a lot my junior year when I was wrestling. I would pray, "If You let me win, I will be good this week." I would win, and when the next match came around, I would pray again. "If You let me win, I will be good next week. I promise." I did not truly know God... I was just bartering with him. Years later, I realized it was more than about winning, which is the small thing. It was about pouring your life into other people to make them successful. That is the big stuff that life is really made of. Like Milton Hershey did for us by putting his success to good use.

I worked out with the team and helped out as much as I could. That year we were invited to the Lehigh Tournament because we had a great team. This was hard for me. To win at Lehigh was my final goal—so close yet so far away.

I set my mind and heart one more time and went to the doctor and laid out my case. My weight class at the end of the year went from 95 to 98 pounds. It did not sound like much, but I asked for one more chance and the doctor said, "Yes." I had not wrestled in competition my whole senior year, but I worked out and kept my weight down as much as I could. I won my wrestle-off, made weight, and earned the right to go to the Lehigh Tournament, representing the ninety-eight-pound weight class. All the tough schools would be there, and individual weight class winners would be crowned as well as an overall team trophy awarded. Here it was, a dream come true. I was heading to Lehigh to represent our school.

I lost my first match and was heartbroken. Tournaments like these are double elimination. I headed down alone to the basement to wrestle for my second match. It was about five minutes until my match. I looked across the gym, and would you believe it? There was Mr. Witman. He was not my coach that year. I did not even know that he was there. He came right to me, and my heart jumped. He once again told me how much he believed in me. I will never forget that day. "There is no fear in love; but perfect love casteth out fear" (I John 4:18a). I wrestled with all the heart and fire I could muster, and I won! I won! I did not win my weight class, but my match scored one point in the year our school brought home the Lehigh Trophy!

When we had our school assembly, I walked up on the platform as we were presented the trophy. I felt my heart would burst because somewhere in that team total was my one point for winning that final wrestling match. I had reached my final goal and was a part of winning the team trophy at the Lehigh Tournament in 1969.

Thirty-five years later, when I walked back into the former Senior Hall auditorium, I could not fight back the tears when I came to the stage and remembered the day our team walked up on that stage to receive that trophy. My dreams had come true. My achievement may not have been lofty in the world's eyes, but to a shy, stricken boy, who was not on the ninth grade wrestling roll call and added him as number 41, it seemed a big deal.

Senior High Auditorium where the Lehigh Trophy
was presented—my only time on this platform.

CHAPTER 8

From Stumbling Block
to Stepping Stone

The music in the sixties had a big effect on me and most of the class of 1969. My friends and I would listen to a DJ out of Philadelphia called Jerry Blavat, "The Boss with the Sauce" and "The Geater with the Heater." We had dance parties in our student home, and girls were brought in. We called our unit parties crazy names like "Action 65." A bunch of us wanted to start a group, and we wrote a song "Life is Not a Bowl Full of Cherries."

The country was at war in Vietnam, and the music reflected the mood and rebellion of the youth of the country. Sometimes, I think the music almost became an escape for guys in our situation. At least it was for me. The music made me think a lot about my life and future, but it did not give me a lot of answers.

Our school choir was the Glee Club, and you had to be good to get in. They sang songs like "Give Me Some Men," "Johnny Smocker," and "Alexander." I envied them because they got to travel all over to represent the school. They got to meet a lot of people, especially girls. The Glee Club was probably the school's best public relations tool. I loved to hear them because they were so good. They would sing almost every Sunday at our chapel service where we would sing some of the great hymns of the faith, whether you liked it or not. I liked it. I just did not understand it. We sang songs like "Oh the Deep, Deep

Love of Jesus," "A Mighty Fortress Is Our God," and "Are Ye Able Said the Master," one of Dr. Clarke E. Hobby's favorites.

We were exposed to all types of music. My favorite through the years was the Alma Mater. I think I sang it literally a thousand times when I was in the school. Maybe not as a class, but as a school the Alma Mater seemed to bind us together as well as the song the Glee Club sang called "Friendship."

Life could be tough at times at Milton Hershey. You laughed at each other, mocked each other, made fun of each other, made up mean nicknames, and even bullied each other. It was a tough pecking order at the student level, and you had to know your spot. It seems to me that when we sang the Alma Mater, for a brief moment we all became one and stuck together like the Spartans of Sparta. We were a band of brothers, and I loved it. I wear my class ring all the time. Through this song the school engraved the great quality of loyalty in my life at that time. They re-worded the Alma Mater after girls entered the school, and I think that is great. Here is the way we sang it when I was there.

Alma Mater
—Milton Hershey School, PA

All hail to thee, Milton Hershey, Thy loyal sons are we;
To stand by thee and each other, Our pledge will ever be.
Thy brown and gold we cherish, and thy traditions dear,
Proudly we'll sing thy praises, for all the world to hear.

Then stand we firmly united, through all the years to come.
By friendship and fond mem'ries of youth and school and home.
We're men of Milton Hershey, and vow to that great name.
Lives filled with strength and honor, to add to Spartan fame.

A great lesson I learned in the Alma Mater is that in any group, you need something to pull people together for a common cause. I have used this concept in coaching and groups of people with whom I work today. It is one of those rare times in life made up of special people with a common background. I mentioned many people in this book, and there are so many more. William Fisher was our high school principal, a homeboy who went on to be our school president. Also, John O'Brien, Tony Colistra, and now Pete Gurt. Others went on to manage HERCO or be on the corporate board or make it in many walks of life and do well in their field and earn the distinction of MHS alumni of the year. As the Alma Mater says "to add to Spartan fame" as well as a host of teachers and faithful workers at Milton Hershey who became honorary alumni, I give them that nod of the head that I learned at Hershey that simply means I respect you.

Milton Hershey's goal was for everyone, including the guys who worked in a factory, taught school, and worked as a salesman or a common laborer. He wanted them to believe they accomplished their goal whatever direction they chose in life. He wanted them to be an asset to society, learn the value of hard work, not ask for a handout, stand up and be counted as men, put their hand out to help others, and find their way with God. If we live lives filled with strength and honor, then we are successful in what we do. I believe this is what Milton Hershey intended for his school and all of its graduates.

As I said before, that is the idealism of Milton Hershey. As I approached graduation, I faced the realism of my experience at Hershey. I had come to appreciate what the school offered, but I wanted out badly. I could hardly wait for June 4, 1969. It was bittersweet. I write this book, especially this part, for my grandchildren—Sawyer, Larynn, Clay, Wayde David, and Wesly—and all who have graduated from Milton Hershey and anyone who comes to a difficult crossroad in life. It is like the last lines of the poem I shared in the beginning of the book. "And each must fashion, ere life is flown, A stumbling block or a Stepping-Stone." I came to a crossroad where my time at Hershey could make my life bitter by my experiences, a stumbling block, or I could somehow process them for good and make them a stepping stone.

I know a number have left Milton Hershey hurt and bitter, and some vow never to go back. Whether we were placed in Hershey due to some unfortunate circumstance beyond our control, we all come to difficult experiences in life and must make one of these two decisions. Please listen to how this part of my story ends.

Graduation—the day they found out
my middle name was Hilary.

It was graduation day, and they called my name, David Hilary Maitland, including the middle name I had hidden for nine years because I was embarrassed by it. They made a mistake and read it a second time. I was the only graduate who had his name repeated; however, I was leaving, and it could not hurt me now. Next I went back to my student home, Rock Ridge. I packed my bags and a suitcase—courtesy of Milton Hershey School as well as $100 for my new start in life. As I walked out the door, I told my houseparent that I hated him. I would never come back and see him again, and I walked away. He was the only person I have ever said that to in my life. I must admit it felt good to say because there was nothing he could do to me.

As I left, everything was a big oxymoron. I was leaving a school that had given me food, clothing, housing, and an education. It was not just all those things—they were all first-class at the expense of someone who shared his wealth in a grateful way. I was walking away in such an ungrateful way. It is not how much we are given that makes us grateful people. It is how we look at the things in life that come our way, good or bad. That will make the difference in our response. On that day, I was not able to process all the good things that could come from all my experiences at Milton Hershey because I was paralyzed by aspects of my situation that caused me to be bitter, which turned to hatred. It was not Milton Hershey's fault that I became an orphan. The school was just trying to be part of the solution. It took me a long time to come to grips with my situation. There are always going to be people above you in the pecking order that you feel are unfair. That will happen in your life for sure. It is how you process it that will make the difference.

I learned years later that acid eats the vessel, and bitterness is like acid. One of the ways to deal with bitterness is to let it go. Ephesians 4:31-32 tells us, "Let all bitterness, and wrath, and anger, and clamour, and evil speaking, be put away from you, with all malice: And be ye kind one to another, tenderhearted, forgiving one another, even as God for Christ's sake hath forgiven you." But I could not do it that day. I chose to hurt with my words and make a vow that I would never come back to the school. That hatred in my heart had sealed my belief that I could never forgive. I was blowing up the bridge and could never cross back over again. I am sad to say today that it felt good to say it because I was never allowed to say it when I was in the school. Even sadder, I wanted the words to hurt my houseparent. My plan was to drive that stake in his heart and walk away. Hurt people, hurt people as that old friend of mine would say.

Have you ever experienced something like this? Haven't we all? In fact, I am sure we have experienced both sides of a story like this, the hurter and the hurtee. We will never stop the hurts in life, but we have to learn how to stop blowing up our bridges in relationships. Maybe you are like I was on that day. I just could not stop the bitterness. I think that day was an accumulation of all the hurts that had come my way in my life up to that point—all the rejection, all the wrongs, and all the unfairness. This houseparent relationship was the straw that broke the camel's back for me. It is funny how I was able to process all the struggle of wrestling and use it to my advantage; but in this area, I succumbed to it and quit. For the next six years, I became a slave to this moment when I let my bitterness finally win.

My brother, Bob, and I, graduation day when
he picked me up in his Corvette.

My brother picked me up on graduation day. As I headed to my brother's car, I felt that I was finally free, but, in fact, it was just the opposite. That moment would haunt me for the next six years. I got in my brother's Corvette. At that time, my brother was the coolest person to me, and he had the coolest car. We drove away for that last trip home. I started my new life. I had met a beautiful girl on my last vacation as a senior; and a few years, later I married her. Over the next six years, I would go back to homecoming but never to Rock Ridge. That day, my problem was that I chose hurt and bitterness. I am sure we have all experienced feelings like this, but the longer they stay, the worse it gets. If you do not process them for good, they will destroy you in the end. People process things like this in different ways. Let me tell you what happened to me.

You and I have to take a hard look at what our goal is in life and evaluate the baggage we take on life's trip. If our goal is money, education, marriage, or being successful in business or trade, when we reach our goal, we will not be satisfied, and no amount of success will take away the hurt and bitterness we carry from the past. It will be like the sixties song, "Is That All There Is?"

I came to that point in my life six years after I graduated from Milton Hershey School. One night, my life changed. I ended up talking to a preacher and told him how I was an orphan, had to go to an orphanage, how hard my life was, and how unhappy I was with life. He took me into his kitchen and gave me tea and crackers. He opened the Bible and told me that I was a sinner and the problem was my heart. He showed me that my bitterness was the problem. He told me that God loved me. I had not felt loved my whole life. He told me that Jesus Christ died on the cross to take away my sins and that I needed to ask for forgiveness and ask God's Son to save me because He was God and He died and rose again. I did just that in a simple prayer, and I became a Christian.

I now began to understand all those songs I sang at Hershey, like "Oh the Deep, Deep Love of Jesus." "Are Ye Able Said the Master." and "Blessed Assurance." I knew what I had to do. I went back that fall and went straight to Rock Ridge and knocked on the door. When my housefather came to the door, I asked, "Do you remember me?" By now, I was six foot two and weighed 230 pounds.

He said, "I remember you."

I asked, "Do you remember what I said to you the day I left?"

He said, "Oh yeah, I remember."

I said, "I have become a Christian, and I would like to ask you for forgiveness for my remark that I hated you and all that I did."

He never asked forgiveness for what he did, but he forgave me. We sat down and talked for an hour and had a good time. When I walked out this time, I was truly free from all the hurt and bitterness. He died a year and a half later.

I plead with you with all my heart to never let bitterness and hatred take root in your heart. "Lest any root of bitterness springing up trouble you, and thereby many be defiled" (Heb. 12:15b). The results in your life will be devastating, and as the verse says, your bitterness will defile others. Many people today—even those who claim to be Christians—are paralyzed by bitterness and hatred. I have found only three ways to overcome bitterness and hatred. First, look diligently to God. Hebrews 12:15a reminds us, "Looking diligently lest any man fail of the grace of God." Second, love abundantly. "And be ye kind one to another, tenderhearted, forgiving one another, even as God for Christ's sake hath forgiven you" (Eph. 4:32). And third, let go daily. "Let all bitterness, and wrath, and anger, and clamour, and evil speaking, be put away from you, with all malice" (Eph. 4:31).

If you do not do these three things, you may punish others; but in the end, the bitterness destroys you. Is it really worth it in the end? It was not for me. I encourage you to get rid of any bitterness you have toward someone before you lose that chance forever.

I then went to find Mr. Don Witman, the man I admired most. When I met him, I told him I had become a Christian. He began to weep and told me he was a Christian when I was in school, but failed to witness to me. I said it was okay, and we wept in joy. Here God put him in my life all along to inspire me. Now that I was a Christian and realized he was, too, all his actions toward me made sense.

Yes, the world is not fair and can be extremely cruel. When we entertain bitterness, we become negative and critical. I am not talking about calling someone out when they need it. That is actually an act of love. Holding people accountable is highly important. John Wooden never screamed or swore at his players, but he demanded much. What is lacking in this negative world is positive encouragement. What Mr. Witman and other people did in my life at Milton Hershey School allowed me to begin to blossom as a person. Our words can be used to build someone up, or they have the potential to destroy the human spirit. I decided in my life to choose the path of praise and encouragement as often as I can. Whether it is in a nickname I use, a quality I see in someone even when they do not see it in themselves, or just looking for the best in someone. I am not talking about flattering. Mr. Witman must have seen something in me that I did not see in myself.

A positive attitude and encouragement are desperately needed in our children today. Proverbs 25:11 says, "A word fitly spoken is like apples of gold in pictures of silver." One of my favorite verses is Ephesians 4:29: "Let no corrupt communication proceed out of your mouth, but that which is good to the use of edifying, that it may minister grace unto the hearers." Grace in that verse means a God-like influence that will reflect in someone's life.

Those few encouraging words to me when I was in the sixth grade novice tournament, when I was in Mr. Witman's office and he showed me the Lehigh trophy from a past year and invited me to shoot for a goal to be part of bringing that trophy back to our great school, got me hooked. I was in.

Can you see the power those words had in the direction of my life? Even Paul in the book of Philippians invites us to join him in his quest for the greatest trophy in the entire universe, the will of God. "I press toward the mark for the prize of the high calling of God in Christ Jesus" (Phil. 3:14).

There are many injustices in this world that come our way. If we are not careful, we will become bitter and not even know it, such as the day I graduated and then took it out on other people. This is painful, but we become what we hate. It is then we cease living and eventually destroy all that is dear to us. We must redeem the past by letting go of bitterness and hatred and pressing toward a trophy much more valuable.

I believe we have two buttons inside us, a giving button and a receiving button. We must not only be positive, think of others rather than ourselves, and be an encourager, but we must also have our receiving button fixed. I find it hard for many people to receive praise or encouragement. Maybe they trusted someone and were hurt, or they have some inverted sense of pride that they must be miserable because that is all they are worth. If they can only see themselves as to how pitiful that looks.

I cannot explain why, but I craved for someone to believe in me. I could not push it away. On the contrary, the encouragement inspired me and drove me to work harder. If someone comes along and sincerely encourages you with no ulterior motive, do not pass up on that chance or drive them away. It may be your last chance at a lifeboat that could take you to safety. The moral of this story is never pass up an opportunity to ask for forgiveness—both with God's Son who died for you and with each other. Christ never passed up an opportunity to share the gospel.

I had turned my stumbling block into a stepping stone. My heart was fully healed, and I am grateful that I went to Milton Hershey. My goal in life is to honor God with my life and to help others. I made the right choice in letting go of the hurt and bitterness. I beg you to do the same no matter what your circumstances are (especially you Hershey graduates). My grandchildren, when you go through hard times, remember Jeremiah 29:11, "For I know the thoughts that I think toward you, saith the Lord, thoughts of peace, and not of evil, to give you an expected end."

As for my brother, the coolest guy I knew, the day he picked me up at Milton Hershey to bring me home was the last day I ever saw him. We chose different pathways in life. He died at the age of fifty-three when he succumbed to alcohol, which became a stumbling block in his life. I guess this is the story of my own little Mt. Everest—how hard the climb was for me, how the hard times made me stronger, and how I met God on the climb up. How I was the blessed one in my family to go to an orphanage called Milton Hershey School.

All hail to thee, Milton Hershey. I thank you for my journey. All praise and honor and glory to the God of heaven. I worship and praise You for all eternity. Thank You for guiding my journey, Jesus Lover of my soul!

CHAPTER 9

Lessons for My Grandchildren

I learned many lessons from the first part of my life's journey that led me to the orphanage, Milton Hershey School. Some I learned along the way, and others I learned years later. They became a part of the fabric of who I am. I also realize I could have stayed a bitter and angry person, or I could overcome my unfortunate circumstances of my early childhood and use the tools Milton Hershey gave me to be a success in my career and station in life, to do good in this world by pulling myself up by the boot straps.

For me, the journey and healing in my life took a deeper vein. I did not want to get to the top of the mountain of my life and be empty and unfulfilled. From an early age, I have always felt a call of destiny in my life. I guess we all want to be famous, to be successful, and to become alumnus of the year. For me, it was something deeper. I wanted to have a great purpose in life. I admired what Milton Hershey did, not so much what he did in the chocolate business, but what he did by starting the school that had a great effect on me. Maybe it was the end of that poem I learned my senior year that haunted me. "Each much fashion, ere life is flown, a stumbling block or a stepping stone." I was like a car engine all torn apart on the shop floor. I had all these experiences, but I did not know how to put them together to make an engine—much less a vehicle to put the engine in to fulfill some grand purpose called life.

I write this part not only to my grandchildren, but to everyone on the planet that is hurting. The only thing that will ever give your life meaning and become the vehicle to put all the parts of your engine, experiences, and circumstances together to make the engine run is a true knowledge of God. That is what was missing in my life. Ecclesiastes 12:13 states, "Let us hear the conclusion of the whole matter: Fear God, and keep his commandments: for this it the whole duty of man."

Six years after I left Milton Hershey, at the age of twenty-three, I became a born-again Christian. From that point on, God became the vehicle for my purpose in life. My viewpoint of all my past experiences changed. I began to see that God had a purpose for every one of them, and He began to put the parts, individual lessons, of my engine together, and He gave my life great meaning by turning the hurts and opportunities that Milton Hershey gave me into great blessings. Here are some of the lessons I learned.

Lesson 1—Life is not fair

As much as you try to make things fair, you would do better to accept the fact that it is not. It can be sometimes, but you better brace yourself. If you do not, you will become bitter and full of hatred and sulk your way through life. Some people have been born with amazing talents, money, personality, circumstances, and station in life. Others do not have as much. Some have great health or emotional drawbacks like shyness or lack of confidence or physical problems. The beautiful, cool, and rich people of this world seem to have an edge. Life is not fair. Seemingly, those who take short cuts in life and do wrong seem to get ahead faster. The Psalmist was frustrated when he wrote Psalm 73:1-16: "Truly God is good to Israel, even to such as are of a clean heart. But as for me, my feet were almost gone; my steps had well-nigh slipped. For there are no bands in their death: but their strength is firm. They are not in trouble as other men; neither are they plagued like other men. Therefore pride compasseth them about as a chain; violence covereth them as a garment. Their eyes stand out with fatness: they have more than heart could wish. They are corrupt, and speak wickedly concerning oppression: they speak loftily. They set their mouth against the heavens, and their tongue walketh through the earth. Therefore his people return hither: and waters of a full cup are wrung out to them. And they say, How doth God know? And is there knowledge in the most High? Behold, these are the ungodly, who prosper in the world; they increase in riches. Verily I have cleansed my heart in vain, and washed my hands in innocency. For all the day long have I been plagued, and chastened every morning. If I say, I will speak thus; behold, I should offend against the generation of thy children. When I thought to know this, it was too painful for me;"

Life is not fair. But I learned through my time at Milton Hershey that the quality, value, and purpose of my life cannot be calculated by whether life is fair. I realized I cannot make life fair, but I can decide my actions and my attitude toward life and affect the outcome of my life as I walk through this unfair minefield of life. I can take the talents I have been given—no matter how small they seem—and use the unfairness as a stepping stone for a great life filled with purpose. My goal eventually became not to make life fair but to recognize life is not fair and focus on making a great life regardless of what I have been given as a person, to use the struggles of life to make me stronger and the blessing of life to make me more grateful.

"Two Frogs in Cream"

Two frogs fell into a can of cream,
  Or so I've heard it told;
The sides of the can were shiny and steep,
  The cream was deep and cold.
"O, what's the use?" croaked Number One,
  "'Tis fate; no help's around.
Goodbye, my friends! Goodbye, sad world!"
  And weeping still, he drowned.
But Number Two, of sterner stuff,
  Dog-paddled in surprise.
The while he wiped his creamy face
  And dried his creamy eyes.
"I'll swim awhile, at least," he said—
  Or so I've heard he said;
"It really wouldn't help the world
  If one more frog were dead."
An hour or two he kicked and swam,
  Not once he stopped to mutter,
But kicked and kicked and swam and kicked,
  Then hopped out, via butter!

  —By T.C. Hamlet
  (Source: www.pathpointers.wordpress.com)

Losing my parents when I was young seemed quite unfair. The hardness of the school seemed unfair. The day I took the swat when they lined us all up seemed unfair. But that is how life goes and that swat only made me stronger and fairer in my judgment today. It made me stronger and more appreciative of things and more compassionate of those less fortunate. I learned to grit through the unfairness and eventually to stop complaining.

The real change in my life came when I received Christ as my Savior, and my whole attitude changed. I reflected retroactively to all the lessons I had learned at school. I learned what the Psalmist learned in Psalm 73:17-19: "Until I went into the sanctuary of God; then understood I their end. Surely thou didst set them in slippery places: thou casted them down into destruction. How are they brought into desolation, as in a moment! They are utterly consumed with terrors."

It doesn't matter if life is fair: that is one of the secrets to life. Many gifted people are in prison, many wealthy people are unhappy, many beautiful people are lonely, and many healthy people are incapacitated by their failures in life. "I returned, and saw under the sun, that the race is not to the swift, nor the battle to the strong, neither yet bread to the wise, nor yet riches to men of understanding, nor yet favour to men of skill; but time and chance happeneth to them all" (Eccles. 9:11). It is not the difficulty of the race or the great abilities given to some to run the race. It is how you run the race that counts and who you run it with. God is a great running partner. Just remember the tortoise did beat the hare in the end. I had to learn to focus on the finish line and not on the obstacles of the race.

Lesson 2—Keep on Bridging

During my first varsity match, when that state champ was bouncing on my chest to pin me, I kept on bridging. I want you to do the same. I have said it many ways in my life, and it is all the same. It is not over until the fat lady sings. If they break your sword, beat them with the handle. The famous words of Winston Churchill, "Never, never, never give up." Or General Douglas MacArthur, "I shall return." Or Vladimir, the great reformer, when he prayed, "Vladimir, Vladimir, doest thou not know the king of England is here. Be careful what you say. Oh Vladimir, Vladimir don't you know the God of heaven is here. Be careful what you say." He preached the truth of the Word of God, and they later burned him at the stake. He went to glory singing. It is not over until it is over.

It was hard work, and it was the discipline of the wrestling room that made me keep on bridging that day. It was my lack of talent that made me work harder. Discipline is a friend to your future. Embrace it and do not shrink back from it. Ask not for the easy road, but work at mastering the rough road. Wrestling tough, cocky Byron Ramsey every Saturday eventually worked in my favor. I made up my mind that night that I was going to keep on bridging. I lost that night with honor, and it became the stepping stone I needed to reach my three goals I set in wrestling.

My dear grandchildren, Sawyer, Larynn, Clay, Wayde David and Wesly, never stop bridging and never give up. You may have to lick your wounds, regroup, take a different approach, and sit under the Juniper tree as Elijah did, but keep on bridging. You never know how it will end.

I have accomplished things people said I could not do, such as when I coached and we won basketball games in the last seconds, coming from far behind. I have had the privilege to speak before thousands of people at one time to share the love of God. I have seen and done things in life that I would have never experienced if I had not kept on bridging. If you ask the Lord, He will help you and give you strength to never give up. "I can do all things through Christ which strengtheneth me" (Philippians 4:13).

The trials and struggles of this life that the Lord allows you to go through will build this type of mindset. I would not be who I am today if it were not for the trials, struggles, and the good discipline I received at Milton Hershey.

Lesson 3—We Will All Be Afraid in Life but Overcome Your Fears

Every one of us has moments we wish we had back in life. They are moments we should have stood up or spoke up for something or someone that we know is right. We feel like the lion in "The Wizard of Oz." For me, it was like that moment in the hallway when that kid said something about my mother. We may never get those moments back, but we can learn from them to help us be ready for those moments in the future. I believe God can give us courage in moments when we need to take a stand. God helps us to overcome our fears before they turn to cowardice. We all have fears we have to overcome such as wrestling Byron Ramsey on those Saturdays when I was afraid because he was so intimidating. We actually became friends, and by facing it straight on, I overcame my fear and he helped me to become a lot better wrestler. When I learned to go out on the wrestling mat and attack by shooting first for the takedown, and when I got the takedown every time after my first match, my fear of crowds went away.

My greatest fear in speaking in front of people was conquered years later when I memorized a verse. 2 Timothy 1:7 reminds us, "For God hath not given us the spirit of fear; but of power, and of love, and of a sound mind." I quoted it many times before I preached my first sermon. When I went into the pulpit, God helped me to overcome my fear of speaking in public. That fear has come back many times, and He has helped me every time. We all fear in life, but our lives cannot be lived to the fullest if we do not overcome our fears. I am saying fears are natural, but we must find a way to overcome them one by one.

Lesson 4—Never Hide from Whom You Really Are

Maybe I was most afraid of what other people thought of me. Hilary seemed to me to be a girl's name, and I was in an all boys' school. People would laugh when they found out, and it would hurt. For a long time I never understood why that was my middle name. We all, at times, want to become what others want us to be or what they think we are, such as the next great ball player, the next great actor, or the next important person. The pressure to match up to other people's ideals can bring a lot of pressure. I felt a lot of this when I was in the school. I was in a 1,500-boy pecking order. No one can ever fully match up to the expectations of the masses. This causes us to pretend a lot or try to become something or someone we are not. Many people hide from whom they are. We wear a mask so people will not find out. I slowly began to learn who I was in the orphanage, what I was good at, what I was not good at, the type of friends I liked to have, and the ones who would accept me for whom I was.

It was a journey that still continues today, but even though I blossomed years later into whom I really was, the foundation of that process was laid at Milton Hershey School. I learned socially where I fit and whom my friends were that I knew I could relate to and count on, and how to be a good friend, and the kind of friend I could be without hiding who I really was. I made my mark small as it was in a sport that was tough and took hard work. Wrestling was one of the disciplines that helped to shape who I am and reveal the real me. I learned that I value loyalty and can be fiercely loyal. I am philosophical to the annoyance of some. I can be quite stubborn when I set a goal, romantic to a fault, and dislike phoniness which I had to face in my own life. I can be lazy, and if it were not for the discipline of Milton Hershey, I would have wasted my life. At the time, I thought all that hard work would kill me. I secretly wanted to be famous, but then I learned to settle with being the best at being me and enjoying the life granted me and the friends I have today.

I learned I have thin skin and that I respond the best to encouragement and fairness. A coach who screamed at me or ignored me because I was not the next best thing made me feel unvalued or devalued. I believe you can get the best out of people with quiet toughness and a lot of encouragement. I learned that although I complained about the school and how tough it was; deep down inside, I wanted discipline and structure like most kids want but will not admit. When people today ask me if I liked the school, I would say, "No. It was hard." Then I would say that it was the best thing in the world for me, and I am forever grateful for my time there. Hebrews 12:11 says, "Now no chastening for the present seemeth to be joyous, but grievous: nevertheless afterward it yieldeth the peaceable fruit of righteousness unto them which are exercised thereby."

The maraschino cherry was when I embraced my name in its totality. My mother gave me my name for a reason. David means "beloved," Hilary was inspired by Sir Edmund Hillary, and Maitland is my father's name, the one good thing he gave me when he helped to bring me into this world.

When I received Christ as my Savior, I took on his name and became a child of God. It completed whom I really am, David Hilary Maitland, a Christian, God's child. Everyone needs to come to terms with whom they are. Then we do not need to hide anymore and pretend we are something we are not.

Lesson 5—Never Lose a Great Friendship

Never let anyone break up a great friendship because you may never get it back the way it was. I have learned that friendships are precious, and the great ones are hard to come by. When we are blessed in life to have something wonderful like a great job, a great family, or a great friendship, be sure that there will be someone who will be jealous. I made a great mistake backing off my friendship with Jerry Doyle because other people thought we were too close as buddies. There are so many people in this world who are not true friends. When we find one or more good friends, we cannot let other opinions get in the way. I made a policy in my life years later: I would be as close to you as you let me. It has never failed me. It has kept me from prejudging people and has allowed me to have friends from many walks of life. Not everyone will have the same beliefs and values, and some may stay away because that is their choice. That is okay. I cannot hide the real me. You never know in what color, shape, size, or personality a true friend comes.

Sometimes, great friendships are found in hard times and conflict or in experiencing a bond because of a common loss (like in an orphanage). Obviously, there are many levels of friendships from acquaintances to best buds to lifelong friends. The greatest friendships are the ones you can share your heart with, get honest counsel from whether you like it or not, and someone you can call on anytime day or night and when your back is up against the wall. They will be there for you. Sometimes, they are only there for a period of time in your life, but their memories last a lifetime. Jerry Doyle, Don Gates, and Jimmy McCauley were three of my best friends. I learned the best way to find a great friend is to be a great friend; and eventually, you will find them or they will find you. Hold onto them as long as you can because they can be some of the brightest spots when life brings some dark and lonely times.

As your grandfather, I will not be around all your lives, but I will be committed to be one of your most loyal friends and will always be there as much as you need me for help, advice, and support. I hope that what I taught you will be a guide and a friend long after I have gone to heaven. "A man that hath friends must shew himself friendly: and there is a friend that sticketh closer than a brother" (Prov. 18:24). Christ has been the best friend to me, and I pray that He will be yours. He has also taught me how to be a better friend to others, so I have been blessed with many great friendships in life.

Lesson 6—Do Not Wait Until the Ball Game is Over

It is not how big your dreams are but that they have value to you when you reach them and that you try to reach them.

- Dream them
- Set them
- Reach them

I remember when Larynn said to Clay when he was little, "Reach for the stars, Clay." It is a great way to live. I learned a great lesson when I was seven and waited for the neighborhood ballgame to be over before I said I wanted to play.

We are not all good at everything, but we all can be good at something. Get out and try, fail, make mistakes, find your niche, conquer your fear, and do not let people or circumstances stop you. You learn through failing or someone saying no. You learn what you are good at and how much you are willing to sacrifice to reach your dream and if it is worth it. The problem is that too many people have their confidence destroyed in the process and quit dreaming.

I needed wrestling more than I ever realized, and though I never tried to be the greatest wrestler in the world, I reached the three simple goals I set. There was a residue of satisfaction and a sense of accomplishment, knowledge, and character from the discipline of wrestling that I will draw on for the rest of my life. I found out what I was made of and realized I could push myself farther than I thought. Diamonds are not formed on the surface but rather you have to dig down deep to find them.

After I was saved, I found the best dreams are the ones that have the greatest eternal value attached to them. Goals with eternal value make the struggle and achievement of those dreams far more satisfying, and they will echo into eternity. My dream may not set the world on fire, but I want my heart to be set on fire because of my dreams. I want to be in the game, and if I have to strike out sometimes, so be it. I lost a lot of matches in the practice room at Hershey before I started winning. If we do not try and get in the game, we are beaten before we start. The most unsettling thought about that is we will never know if we could have done it. We may change dreams, but that is not quitting. That is searching for your gifts and purpose. When you stop dreaming, or are not willing to pay the price for your dreams, that is quitting.

We have two problems in America. The first is we never start dreaming, we never get in the game. The second is we quit too early on good dreams. Failure and struggles may be the potting soil that makes your dreams grow. It was that way for Thomas Edison, Albert Einstein, and Abraham Lincoln. I taught your mom to never be a quitter. Get in the game and reach for the stars!

Lesson 7—Encourage, Praise, and Inspire

When I was in sixth grade and wrestled in the novice wrestling tournament, Mr. Witman's one phrase to me eventually changed my destiny at Milton Hershey. "Dave, someday you are going to be a great wrestler." It was not that I took it literally. It was that he encouraged me. He praised and inspired me.

I saw a lot of bullying in my life, a lot of teasing that was hurtful, and nicknames that could tear at the human confidence. It is because we live in a cruel world and all the posters on the walls are not going to change it. It is a choice you make, Mr. Witman made, and I, too, was to make. It is the choice to encourage people, praise people, and try to inspire them to become more than what they think they can be.

Later in life, after I graduated from the orphanage, I was working a job trying to find my niche in life, and a lawyer said to me, "What's a guy like you doing working in a place like this?"

It was not that I was working in a bad place. He saw something in me that I could not see in myself.

I asked him, "Why? What do you mean?"

He said, "You have too much talent to be working here."

I was so encouraged and inspired by his praise. I put in my two weeks' notice and quit my job. I put on a suit, went up town, and went to every bank until I got a job. The man I met that worked in the bank I got a job at would eventually help me find my calling in life. Our words can be so cutting and downright sinful. Ephesians 4:29 tells us, "Let no corrupt communication proceed out of your mouth, but that which is good to the use of edifying, that it may minister grace unto the hearers." Mr. Witman and that lawyer chose to edify or build up with their words. That is what I chose to do for myself and for others. The benefits in my life and others have been incredible. You may not even realize how powerful your words can be to change someone's direction. I have never seen that lawyer again, and I wonder if he ever realized how his praise encouraged and inspired me.

Everyone had nicknames in school. Some of the ones for me were mean. I wanted the nickname Spiderman because I was so skinny from pulling weight. That nickname was more inspiring, and it caught on. In Anne of Green Gables, she asked to be called Cordelia, which seemed to be more inspiring when she went to live with Matthew and Marilla. She said, "If you can't call me Cordelia, at least call me Anne with an 'E' on the end which sounds more romantic." We should live that way all the time, but it is a lot of work to train yourself to put others' best interests first. I guess the Bible calls it love in I Corinthians 13:5, "Love doth not behave itself unseemly, seeketh not her own, is not easily provoked, thinketh no evil."

My prayer is that someday some encouragement or praise that I have said to you may inspire you to achieve great things in your life. Then pass it on to all the people you can like Don Witman and the lawyer did for me. If you choose to live this way, the rewards in your life will be amazing. I know that I have experienced it.

Lesson 8—Understand the Pecking Order of Life

At Milton Hershey there were many pecking orders. Any time you have more than one person you have a pecking order. I believe it is God ordained because of the need for order. You have to understand it, know where you fit into it, and how to handle it if you are elevated in that order. Some boys in our school never seemed to get it and got beaten up a lot or lost friends because they did not know there is a time to keep your mouth shut, to listen and learn. I am not sure how I learned it, but I learned it quickly. My shyness probably kept me quiet until I learned by other's actions, and that worked in my favor. In the end the leaders, good and bad, seemed to work their way to the top. The goal is not getting to the top, but knowing where you stand in the order and how you can use your position to help others in the pecking order.

Rule one in the pecking order is to let another man praise you. I have found that people who brag about themselves are often lower in the pecking order than what they think. When I did well in wrestling, someone said, "Hey, Maitland, pretty good." That raised my place in the pecking order.

Rule two is go to the back of the banquet room and get called up rather than go to the front and be asked to move to the back. If you lose your standing in the pecking order, it is embarrassing. I never had that luxury when my number was forty-one on the depth chart out of forty. That is not even in the back of the banquet room. That is sitting out in the hallway. I worked my way up from the bottom, and when I was called upon, I tried to be ready, like when Joseph was called from the prison (which is the bottom of the pecking order in Egypt) and rose to second in the pecking order. He did it by being prepared rather than self-promotion. Pharaoh said who is better prepared than Joseph and up he came.

Rule three is God runs and is the head of all pecking orders. "By me kings reign, and princes decree justice. By me princes rule, and nobles, even all the judges of the earth" (Prov. 8:15-16). Remember that! God can promote you in the pecking order like Joseph or demote you like Saul anytime He wants. The true status of your position in any pecking order is not dictated by other people but by God. God uses the pecking order for His purposes.

Rule four, the best way to move up the pecking order is to serve others. The worst way to move up the pecking order is to take advantage of them. You will probably see them on the way down, and it will not be pleasant. The pecking order is where you fit in the scheme of things in life and how much influence you have in any group of which you a part. I often think of it as one of the ways God uses, for you to have purpose and fulfill His will. In short, learn your place in the pecking order of life and use it to bring glory to God. You will never regret it.

Lesson 9—Home is Where You Hang Your Heart

When I became an orphan, I lost my home and for many years became a nomad and never really felt that I had a permanent home. My aunt's place was home when I was on vacation from Hershey, and Milton Hershey was home until I graduated from high school. The bus rides showed me I was a wanderer, and I longed to belong to some place and someone. I believe many, if not all the kids who feel rejected and abandoned, feel the same way. I came to realize that home is where I wanted it to be and where I decided I would hang my heart or where I wanted to be most. We all end up where our heart is. Remember that! Matthew 6:21 states, "For where your treasure is, there will your heart be also."

The prodigal son left home because his heart was somewhere else, and it cost him dearly. It cost him all that he had. He returned home because that is where he realized his heart really needed to be. When I truly received Christ, I found an eternal home in heaven, and I cherish what I call home here on earth. That is being with the people I love and hold as my treasure. Because of all those bus rides and my nomadic journey at Hershey, I cherish where I hang my heart every day. Do not take anything for granted. Say I love you often to the ones who mean the most to you and put your time, money, and efforts into the things you love and the people you love. You will not have to go anywhere because you will be home every day. Even when you finish this life, you will be home. Always be grateful and cherish where your heart is, and may your heart be committed to the Lord because then you will always feel like you are home wherever you are.

Lesson 10—Life Can be Cruel

Do not let anyone make you feel stupid about yourself without your permission. There are only two people who can stop you from becoming all you need to be in life. That is you and other people. There is only one person who can help you become all you need to be in life, and that is Christ. "I can do all things through Christ which strengtheneth me" (Phil. 4:13).

We defeat ourselves when we quit and take the easy way out. We fail when we let the cruel opinions of others stop us. That one coach who called me a scared rabbit when I lost at a wrestling scrimmage hurt me so deeply. I wanted to quit, but I kept going and eventually reached my goals. People can say the meanest things to hurt other people. I often feel a teacher, husband, wife, mother, or father hold the spirit of another person in their hands and can crush that person in one statement. I beg of you to watch your words so that you do not become the person who destroys someone by your words and don't allow yourself to be destroyed by another's words.

You must build confidence in what you believe you can do and not on what others think you cannot do. Saul did not think David could kill Goliath. I am sure some people thought that Sir Edmund Hillary could not climb Mt. Everest. I cannot stop life from dealing you some cruel blows, but I can tell you that you do not have to let people make you feel stupid about yourself unless you give them permission. Just because someone said you are stupid or calls you a scared rabbit does not mean you are stupid and that you cannot overcome your fear. Do not listen to people like this. If there is no truth to what they say, then let it go and move on; and if there is truth, then use it as a stepping stone; do not let it destroy you. Many people have no confidence in what they can do because other people have convinced them they cannot, so they live defeated lives. They have no right to do that. Life can be cruel, but God loves you and you can be anything He wants you to be. I refuse to let people or myself put me in a box. "Then said David to the Philistine, Thou comest to me with a sword, and with a spear, and with a shield: but I come to thee in the name of the Lord of hosts, the God of the armies of Israel, whom thou hast defied" (1 Sam. 17:45). David refused to let people do that to him. Know your strengths and weaknesses. Put your confidence in the Lord as David did, and other people will not be able to dictate what you can or cannot do. The Lord will.

Lesson 11—Let All Bitterness and Hatred Go

I saved this for last because it was my hardest lesson to learn. You are going to have hard times in life, and life will not always be fair. Bitterness can spring up in your life in a thousand ways. You have to learn how to forgive and let it go, or it will destroy you in the end. I shared with you all my rough times I had starting with the death of my parents. I held on to all my hurts way too long. It came to a head when I told my houseparent how much I hated him when I left the school after graduation. It ate away at me like cancer. There are homeboys and girls today who still cannot let go of the bitterness for all the injustices they endured while at Milton Hershey. If bitterness has not destroyed them yet, it eventually will. It is not just in the orphanage but also in churches, workplaces, and families.

I first learned to forgive and to let go when I asked forgiveness from God for my sins, and then I could let go of the hurts I received from others. "And be ye kind one to another, tenderhearted, forgiving one another, even as God for Christ's sake hath forgiven you" (Eph. 4:32). That is why I forgive and cannot hold grudges and why I went back to apologize to my houseparent even though he never asked for my forgiveness. I was free from bitterness and the poison it brings.

Learn to seek forgiveness and to grant forgiveness, and you may have learned one of the greatest lessons in life. The greatest is love, and I love all five of you, Sawyer, Larynn, Clay, Wayde David, and Wesly.

Love, Papa

CHAPTER 10

Hope for the Hurting

To those who feel abandoned:

My abandonment was something I felt to be irreversible. My parents died, and I could never change that. Maybe you have a similar situation, or maybe your parents got a divorce or gave you up for adoption because they couldn't care for you or, sad to say, did not want you. Hurts doesn't it? You wonder why God doesn't do something to fix it. You feel like the little boy who walked into my office one day and pulled out all the change he had in his pocket, laid it on my desk, and said, "I want to buy my parents back together again." True story! Sometimes parents say, "It's better for the kids if we break up." Parents might say that, but the children don't. Many times the children feel it's their fault, and they feel betrayed and abandoned.

What if you are adopted whether it is from another country or you have been given up by your family? Even if you're in a loving family and have all the food, clothes, schooling like I had at Milton Hershey, one day, you still will have to work through these feelings of abandonment and get some answers to these questions: Why didn't they want me? Where are they now? Why did God have to take them? Although I have everything I need, why am I unhappy?

First, it's not your fault. It may be a different case if you're an adult and you have chosen the wrong path in life, but it was not my fault my parents died. I had nothing to do with it, and you shouldn't blame yourself for your parents' divorce. It's not your fault that you were adopted because someone couldn't provide for you or didn't want you. You may feel like a casualty of a life that is not fair, but you are not the cause of it.

Second, it's not God's fault. God has allowed this in your life, but you must remember: "It is not God's fault." You may not understand what I am going to say to you right now, but it is true. God says in the Bible that He will be a Father to the fatherless. This means that God has a special plan for you (Jer. 29:11).

Like Moses in the bulrushes, God will turn these apparent stumbling blocks in life into stepping stones if you will let Him. You may feel abandoned, but He sees you as special. There is hope!

To those who have great insecurities:

We all have insecurities. Some of us cover them up better than others. My major insecurities were painful shyness and lack of courage. Once again, it is not God's fault we have these. God allows us to have them, and there are thousands of different insecurities that we need to overcome in order to become strong in our character. In fact, God says that He will help you overcome them. 2 Corinthians 12:9a says, "And he [God] said unto me, My grace is sufficient for thee: for my strength is made perfect in weakness." Don't make excuses for your fears and shortcomings in life, but rather face them one by one. If I can become a better wrestler by Byron Ramsey throwing me around like a rag doll, then there is hope for you. Maybe it's time to go against the wind and the tide and start believing you can. Maybe you need someone to believe in you.

To those who struggle with the past:

Maybe you have trouble dealing with your past. Bitterness has rooted very deep in your life over the years. Maybe it is like the root of that dandelion I had to dig out with that long dandelion tool. The dandelion had a deep root called a "tap" root, and you had to use that long tool to get the entire root out or else it would grow back. Bitterness will have a big "tap" root and will cause anger and hatred, and if you don't dig it out of your life, bitterness will affect your future as well as your future relationships. Because of what has happened, you may feel like damaged goods, and you may feel trapped by your past.

First, there is hope for you! You don't have to live this way! Reach out to someone who will help you.

Second, don't let your past dictate your future. Learn how to use your past and turn it from a stumbling block to a stepping stone. The secret is to harness your past rather than be shackled by it.

Third, you have to learn to let go. If you don't let go, you are in danger of becoming what you hate. I hope that this book shows it is never too late to repair a broken relationship—no matter whom it may be with.

There is one more lesson I learned one lonely night years after the events recorded in this book had taken place. You can't do it on your own, you need God. I realized my broken relationship with God had to be fixed so that I could have peace with God, myself, and with others. My healing had to start within me just like it did with that sinner who had a broken relationship with God and gave us one of the sweetest hymns of redemption and healing. I leave its simple word with you as a prayer.

"Amazing Grace"

Amazing grace how sweet the sound,
That saved a wretch like me.
I once was lost but now I'm found
T'was blind but now I see.

—By John Newton, 1829

If you are hurting, there is hope! Please talk to someone that will help you with your broken relationship with God. God has a plan for you for healing because He is the only one who knows how to turn the stumbling blocks in your life into stepping stones. If you can't find anyone to help you, contact me at srbaptistcamp@aol.com, and I will help you find the answers you need.

This was only the beginning of healing and hope for me. If I write again, I want to tell of the great purpose and meaning He gave to me in the years that would follow. That healing has led me to an incredible life, a life you can have also.

Abandoned no more,
Hilary

About the Author

It's now been 38 years that the author has been a preacher. Many in his ministry call him P.D. (short for Pastor Dave). His mother gave him the name Hilary for a special reason and prayed that he would be a preacher someday, which is the reason for the pen name for this book—PD Hilary.

> "You don't have to be a fantastic hero to do certain things—to compete you can just be an ordinary chap, sufficiently motivated to reach challenging goals."
> —Sir Edmund Hillary

The author has found his place in life and feels abandoned no more. Just an ordinary chap who rose to the expectation of a mother's prayers by the grace of God. His years at Milton Hershey helped him on the journey from stumbling block to stepping stone.

The author hopes that this book is a help in your journey in life.

CPSIA information can be obtained
at www.ICGtesting.com
Printed in the USA
BVHW032350110419
545322BV00001B/1/P